FIRST PAST THE POST®

English:
Spelling, Punctuation & Grammar

Multiple Choice

Book 1

How to use this book to make the most of 11 plus exam preparation

It is important to remember that for 11 plus exams there is no national syllabus, no pass mark and no retake option. It is therefore vital that your child is fully primed to perform to the best of their ability so that they give themselves the best possible chance on the day.

English: Spelling, Punctuation & Grammar

This topic-based workbook is tailored towards the question styles included in the last three sections of the standard Granada Learning (GL) English test. The mixed tests at the end of the book are designed to provide timed practice.

Never has it been more useful to learn from mistakes!

Students can improve by as much as 15%, not only by focused practice, but also by targeting any weak areas.

How to manage your child's practice

To get the most up-to-date information, visit our website, www.elevenplusexams.co.uk, the UK's largest online resource for 11 plus, with over 65,000 webpages and a forum administered by a select group of experienced moderators.

About the authors

The Eleven Plus Exams' **First Past The Post®** series has been created by a team of experienced tutors and authors from leading British universities.

Published by: Technical One Ltd t/a Eleven Plus Exams

With special thanks to all the children who tested our material at the ElevenPlusExams centre in Harrow.

ISBN: 978-1-912364-21-3

Copyright © ElevenPlusExams.co.uk 2018

Second edition

About Us

At Eleven Plus Exams, we supply high-quality 11 plus tuition for your children. Our free website at **www.elevenplusexams.co.uk** is the largest website in the UK that specifically prepares children for the 11 plus exams. We also provide online services to schools and our **First Past The Post®** range of books has been well-received by schools, tuition centres and parents.

Eleven Plus Exams is recognised as a trusted and authoritative source. We have been quoted in numerous national newspapers, including *The Telegraph*, *The Observer*, the *Daily Mail* and *The Sunday Telegraph*, as well as on national television (BBC1 and Channel 4), and BBC radio.

Our website offers a vast amount of information and advice on the 11 plus, including a moderated online forum, books, downloadable material and online services to enhance your child's chances of success. Set up in 2004, the website grew from an initial 20 webpages to more than 65,000 today, and has been visited by millions of parents. It is moderated by experts in the field, who provide support for parents both before and after the exams.

Don't forget to visit **www.elevenplusexams.co.uk** and see why we are the market's leading one-stop shop for all your 11 plus needs. You will find:

- ✓ Comprehensive quality content and advice written by 11 plus experts

- ✓ Eleven Plus Exams online shop supplying a wide range of practice books, e-papers, software and apps

- ✓ Lots of FREE practice papers to download

- ✓ Professional tuition service

- ✓ Short revision courses

- ✓ Year-long 11 plus courses

- ✓ Mock exams tailored to reflect those of the main examining bodies

Other Titles in the First Past The Post® Series

11+ Essentials Range of Books

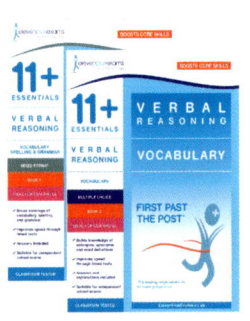
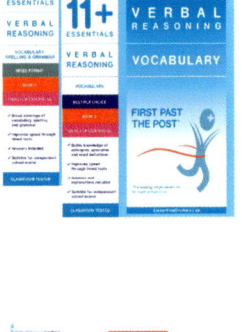

978-1-912364-60-2	Verbal Reasoning: Cloze Tests Book 1 - Mixed Format
978-1-912364-61-9	Verbal Reasoning: Cloze Tests Book 2 - Mixed Format
978-1-912364-78-7	Verbal Reasoning: Cloze Tests Book 3 - Mixed Format
978-1-912364-79-4	Verbal Reasoning: Cloze Tests Book 4 - Mixed Format
978-1-912364-62-6	Verbal Reasoning: Vocabulary Book 1 - Multiple Choice
978-1-912364-63-3	Verbal Reasoning: Vocabulary Book 2 - Multiple Choice
978-1-912364-64-0	Verbal Reasoning: Vocabulary Book 3 - Multiple Choice
978-1-912364-65-7	Verbal Reasoning: Vocabulary, Spelling and Grammar Book 1 - Multiple Choice
978-1-912364-66-4	Verbal Reasoning: Vocabulary, Spelling and Grammar Book 2 - Multiple Choice
978-1-912364-68-8	Verbal Reasoning: Vocabulary in Context Level 1
978-1-912364-69-5	Verbal Reasoning: Vocabulary in Context Level 2
978-1-912364-70-1	Verbal Reasoning: Vocabulary in Context Level 3
978-1-912364-71-8	Verbal Reasoning: Vocabulary in Context Level 4
978-1-912364-74-9	Verbal Reasoning: Vocabulary Puzzles Book 1
978-1-912364-75-6	Verbal Reasoning: Vocabulary Puzzles Book 2
978-1-912364-76-3	Verbal Reasoning: Practice Papers Book 1 - Multiple Choice

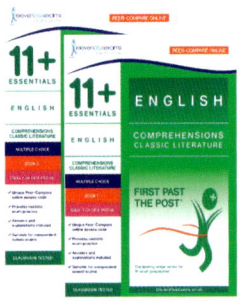

978-1-912364-02-2	English: Comprehensions Classic Literature Book 1 - Multiple Choice
978-1-912364-05-3	English: Comprehensions Contemporary Literature Book 1 - Multiple Choice
978-1-912364-08-4	English: Comprehensions Non-Fiction Book 1 - Multiple Choice
978-1-912364-14-5	English: Mini Comprehensions - Inference Book 1
978-1-912364-15-2	English: Mini Comprehensions - Inference Book 2
978-1-912364-16-9	English: Mini Comprehensions - Inference Book 3
978-1-912364-11-4	English: Mini Comprehensions - Fact-Finding Book 1
978-1-912364-12-1	English: Mini Comprehensions - Fact-Finding Book 2
978-1-912364-21-3	English: Spelling, Punctuation and Grammar Book 1
978-1-912364-00-8	English: Practice Papers Book 1 - Multiple Choice
978-1-912364-17-6	Creative Writing Examples

978-1-912364-30-5	Numerical Reasoning: Quick-Fire Book 1
978-1-912364-31-2	Numerical Reasoning: Quick-Fire Book 2
978-1-912364-32-9	Numerical Reasoning: Quick-Fire Book 1 - Multiple Choice
978-1-912364-33-6	Numerical Reasoning: Quick-Fire Book 2 - Multiple Choice
978-1-912364-34-3	Numerical Reasoning: Multi-Part Book 1
978-1-912364-35-0	Numerical Reasoning: Multi-Part Book 2
978-1-912364-36-7	Numerical Reasoning: Multi-Part Book 1 - Multiple Choice
978-1-912364-37-4	Numerical Reasoning: Multi-Part Book 2 - Multiple Choice

978-1-912364-43-5	Mathematics: Mental Arithmetic Book 1
978-1-912364-44-2	Mathematics: Mental Arithmetic Book 2
978-1-912364-45-9	Mathematics: Worded Problems Book 1
978-1-912364-46-6	Mathematics: Worded Problems Book 2
978-1-912364-52-7	Mathematics: Worded Problems Book 3
978-1-912364-47-3	Mathematics: Dictionary Plus
978-1-912364-50-3	Mathematics: Crossword Puzzles Book 1
978-1-912364-51-0	Mathematics: Crossword Puzzles Book 2
978-1-912364-48-0	Mathematics: Practice Papers Book 1 - Multiple Choice

978-1-912364-87-9	Non-Verbal Reasoning: 2D Book 1 - Multiple Choice
978-1-912364-88-6	Non-Verbal Reasoning: 2D Book 2 - Multiple Choice
978-1-912364-85-5	Non-Verbal Reasoning: 3D Book 1 - Multiple Choice
978-1-912364-86-2	Non-Verbal Reasoning: 3D Book 2 - Multiple Choice
978-1-912364-83-1	Non-Verbal Reasoning: Practice Papers Book 1 - Multiple Choice

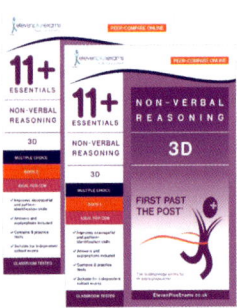

Contents

This workbook comprises three topic-based chapters and three mixed tests. Each chapter comprises 15 exercises, and each mixed test comprises three exercises.

Instructions

For spelling and punctuation questions, circle the letter corresponding to the group of words containing an error. If there is no mistake, circle N. For grammar questions, circle the letter corresponding to the most appropriate word or group of words so that the passage makes sense.

Examples

Find the group of words containing the **spelling** error and circle the corresponding letter. **If there is no error, circle N.**

Example 1

Technology has evolved at an alarming rate over the past century.

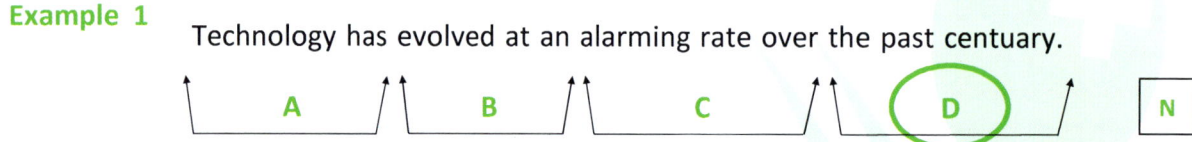

Find the group of words containing the error in the use of **punctuation**, including the use of **capital letters**, and circle the corresponding letter. **If there is no error, circle N.**

Example 2

"I can't believe you lost your mothers ring!" exclaimed Lucy's friend.

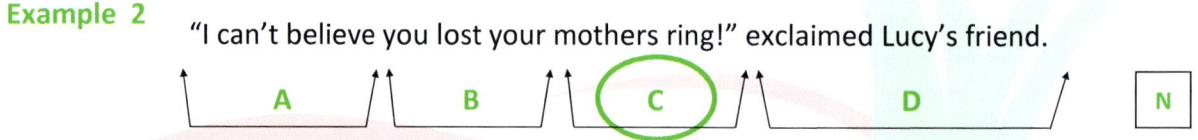

Find the word or group of words that best completes the passage and circle the corresponding letter.

Example 3

The sharp, odorous

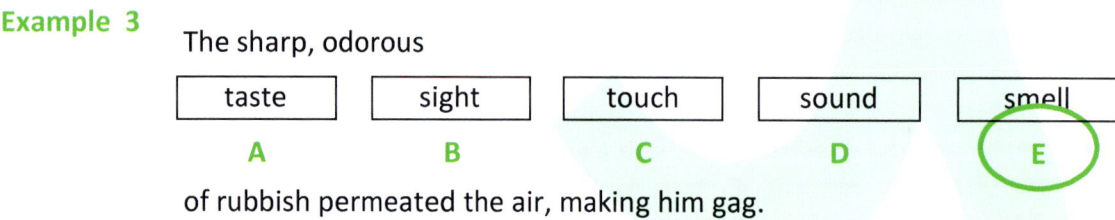

of rubbish permeated the air, making him gag.

Answers

To mark your work, use the 'Answers & Explanations' section at the back of this book. The mark scheme will tell you the correct answer option as well as a short explanation of why this is the case.

Question	Answer	Explanation
Example 1	D	The incorrectly spelt word is '**century**' — the correct spelling is '**century**'.
Example 2	C	Missing possessive apostrophe in '**mother's**'.
Example 3	E	The correct word is '**smell**': 'The sharp, odorous **smell** of rubbish permeated...'

Common Spelling Errors

Spotting spelling errors is largely dependent on a strong vocabulary and familiarity with the words. However, there are certain spelling rules that can be observed to avoid common errors.

Common errors that occur relate to:

- Silent letters, e.g. **k**night, We**d**nesday, autum**n**

- Complex plurals, e.g. box → box**es**, hal**f** → hal**ves**, countr**y** → countr**ies**

- 'ie' vs. 'ei' - although there are exceptions, the rule is usually 'i before e, except after c', e.g. bel**ie**f, rec**ei**ve, rel**ie**ve

- Differentiating between common suffixes, e.g. -**able** and -**ible**, -**ant** and -**ent**

- Words that become another word when a letter is added, changed or removed, but are incorrect in the context of the sentence, e.g. **k**now → now , le**a**d → led

Common Punctuation Errors

Familiarise yourself with the correct use of all types of punctuation, including capital letters. There are some common errors which are often found in these types of exercises:

- Punctuation must always come inside of the closing speech mark:

- ✗ "We're going on holiday"**.**

- ✔ "We're going on holiday**.**"

  The opposite applies to brackets: punctuation should not be in the brackets, unless the brackets contain a complete sentence, e.g. I hope you have a lovely birthday **(**and holiday**)!**

- Capital letters must be used appropriately, i.e. only for the start of sentences or proper nouns.

- Recognise the difference between colons and semicolons, and understand when they are used.

- Understand the appropriate use of apostrophes: they are only used to indicate a contraction of two words or possession. Take particular care with apostrophes attached to plural words, e.g. children**'s** or countr**ies'**.

- Only use commas when appropriate. Very generally, this is when you would take a breath when reading aloud.

Common Grammar Errors

- Make sure verbs are correctly conjugated, e.g. 'This morning, I **walked** the dog.' or 'This morning, I **will walk** the dog.'

- Select the word in the correct tense so that it is consistent with the rest of the sentence.

BLANK PAGE

FIRST PAST THE POST®

Spelling

Spelling - Exercise 1

The passage below contains some **spelling** errors. On each line, there is either **one** error or **no** error. Find the group of words containing the error and circle the corresponding letter beneath. **If there is no error, circle N.**

Pluto

1 After its discovery in 1930, Pluto was classified initialy as the ninth

    A   B   C   D   N

2 closest planet orbitting the Sun. However, in 2006, the International

    A   B   C   D   N

3 Astronomical Union (IAU) demoted it to the status of a dwarve planet,

    A   B   C   D   N

4 after discoveries of similiar-sized objects in the Kuiper Belt. The

    A   B   C   D   N

5 contentious decision followed eight days of debates, with the final

    A   B   C   D   N

6 result based on Pluto's failure to meet the formel definition of a

    A   B   C   D   N

7 planet. However, the desision was met with great uproar amongst the

    A   B   C   D   N

8 public; even now there are campaigns and petetions to overturn it.

    A   B   C   D   N

Spelling - Exercise 2

The passage below contains some **spelling** errors. On each line, there is either **one** error or **no** error. Find the group of words containing the error and circle the corresponding letter beneath. **If there is no error, circle N.**

Dear Mr Hartley

1 I am writing to you to strongly condem your decision to remove

    A   B   C   D   N

2 swimming lessons from the curriculum. Swimming is an enjoyable

    A   B   C   D   N

3 way of staying healthy, and our regular, friendly competitons with

    A   B   C   D   N

4 other schools helps fostor community spirit. Although the local pool

    A   B   C   D   N

5 has shut down, I beleive the school has sufficient funds to allocate

    A   B   C   D   N

6 toowards building a pool. The remainder of the cost can be covered

    A   B   C   D   N

7 by holding fundraising events, colecting donations from alumni and

    A   B   C   D   N

8 hireing out the pool during the school holidays. I hope you consider

    A   B   C   D   N

my views, and thank you for taking the time to read my letter.

Lucy Baker

Spelling - Exercise 3

The passage below contains some **spelling** errors. On each line, there is either **one** error or **no** error. Find the group of words containing the error and circle the corresponding letter beneath. **If there is no error, circle N.**

An extract from 'The Hound of the Baskervilles' by Arthur Conan Doyle

1 A low moan had fallen upon our ears. Their it was again upon

A   B   C   D   N

2 our left! On that side a ridge of rocks ended in a sheer cliff which

A   B   C   D   N

3 overlooked a stone-strewn slope. On its jaged face was spread-

A   B   C   D   N

4 eagled some dark, iregular object. As we ran towards it the

A   B   C   D   N

5 vague outline hardened into a definate shape. It was a prostrate

A   B   C   D   N

6 man face downward upon the ground, the head doubled under

A   B   C   D   N

7 him at a horrible angel, the shoulders rounded and the body

A   B   C   D   N

8 hunched together as if in the act of throwing a somersalt.

A   B   C   D   N

Spelling - Exercise 4

The sentences below contain some **spelling** errors. Each sentence has either **one** error or **no** error. Find the group of words containing the error and circle the corresponding letter beneath. **If there is no error, circle N.**

Sentences: Non-Fiction

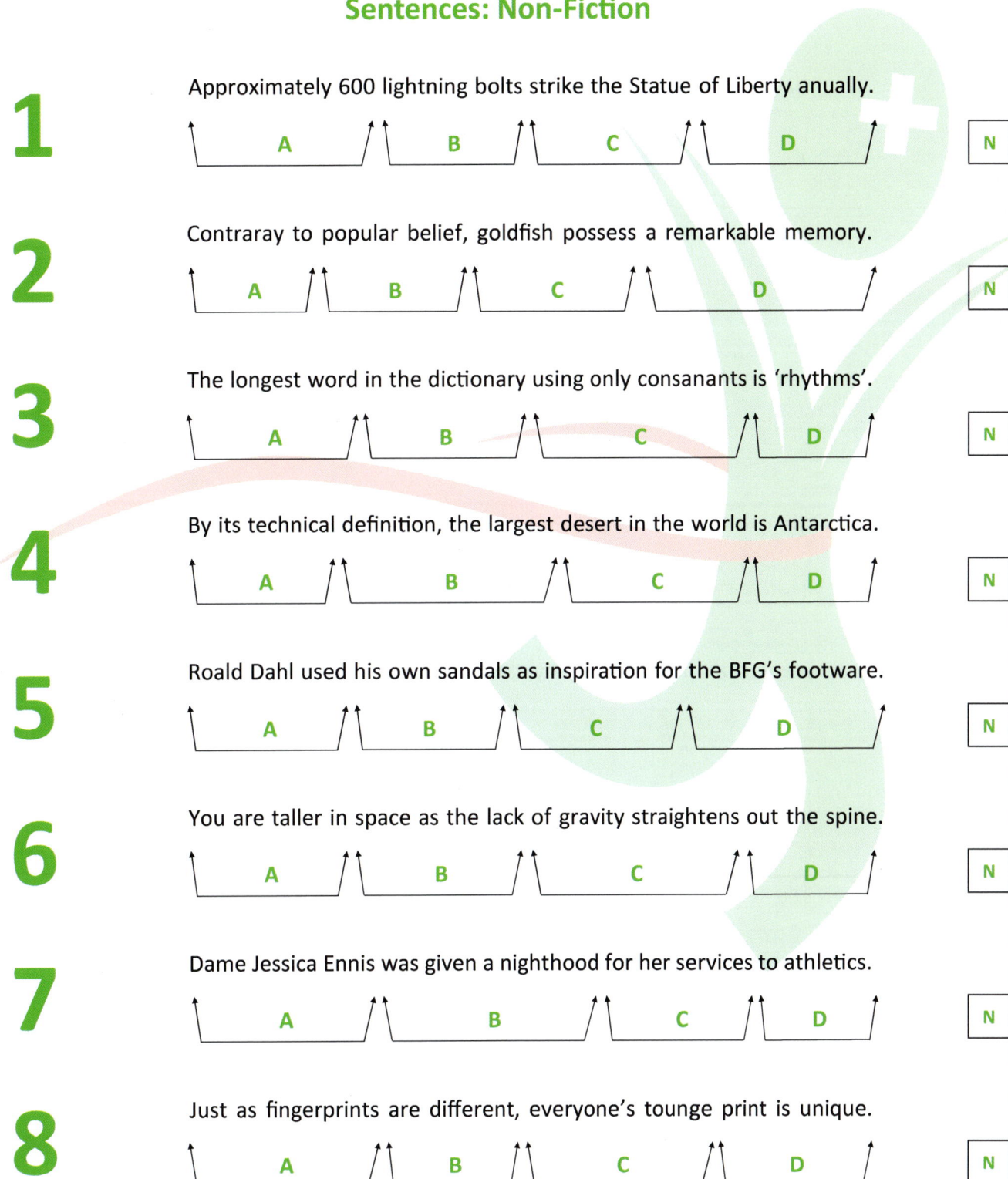

1. Approximately 600 lightning bolts strike the Statue of Liberty anually.

    A   B   C   D   N

2. Contraray to popular belief, goldfish possess a remarkable memory.

    A   B   C   D   N

3. The longest word in the dictionary using only consanants is 'rhythms'.

    A   B   C   D   N

4. By its technical definition, the largest desert in the world is Antarctica.

    A   B   C   D   N

5. Roald Dahl used his own sandals as inspiration for the BFG's footware.

    A   B   C   D   N

6. You are taller in space as the lack of gravity straightens out the spine.

    A   B   C   D   N

7. Dame Jessica Ennis was given a nighthood for her services to athletics.

    A   B   C   D   N

8. Just as fingerprints are different, everyone's tounge print is unique.

    A   B   C   D   N

Spelling - Exercise 5

The passage below contains some **spelling** errors. On each line, there is either **one** error or **no** error. Find the group of words containing the error and circle the corresponding letter beneath. **If there is no error, circle N.**

Furry Fiasco

1 Claire was naturally ecxited when Ruby invited her for a sleepover.

    A   B   C   D   N

2 Although Ruby had warned her about the overwelming number of

    A   B   C   D   N

3 pets she had, given her friend's tendancy to exaggerate, Claire hadn't

    A   B   C   D   N

4 thought much of it. So when the self-proclaimed 'animal hater' was

    A   B   C   D   N

5 greeted at the entranse by three puppies, five kittens and twelve

    A   B   C   D   N

6 hamsters, the only logical reaction was to sprint out of the house

    A   B   C   D   N

7 screaming—or so she thought. It turned out that Claire's hatered of

    A   B   C   D   N

8 animals was simply misgided fear, but neither Ruby nor her family ever

    A   B   C   D   N

let Claire forget about that first visit.

Spelling - Exercise 6

The passage below contains some **spelling** errors. On each line, there is either **one** error or **no** error. Find the group of words containing the error and circle the corresponding letter beneath. **If there is no error, circle N.**

Giant Pandas

1 Native to China, giant pandas are distinguished by their distinctiv

A   B   C   D   N

2 black and white fur. They lead a predominantly solitary life, inhabiting

A   B   C   D   N

3 bambo forests in mountainous areas. However, less than 2,000

A   B   C   D   N

4 pandas remane in the wild, due to deforestation for agriculture and

A   B   C   D   N

5 infastructure. This directed the conservation organisation, the World

A   B   C   D   N

6 Wide Fund for Nature, to increace efforts to protect pandas and their

A   B   C   D   N

7 habitats; their work in recent years has been successful in

A   B   C   D   N

8 downgrading the extinction risk from 'endangered' to 'vunerable'.

A   B   C   D   N

Spelling - Exercise 7

The sentences below contain some spelling errors. Each sentence has either one error or no error. Find the group of words containing the error and circle the corresponding letter beneath. **If there is no error, circle N.**

Sentences from 'The Wonderful Wizard of Oz' by L. Frank Baum

1 Birds with rare and brilliant plummage sang and fluttered in the trees.

    A   B   C   D   N

2 The Tin Woodman gave a sigh of satisfaction and lowerd his axe.

    A   B   C   D   N

3 The waiting was tirsome and wearing, and at last they grew vexed.

    A   B   C   D   N

4 So the Wizad unfastened his head and emptied out the straw.

    A   B   C   D   N

5 "I am terribly afriad of falling, myself," said the Cowardly Lion.

    A   B   C   D   N

6 They went to bed quiet early and slept soundly until daylight...

    A   B   C   D   N

7 "Go to the strangers and sting them to death!" commanded the Witch.

    A   B   C   D   N

8 The wicked woman was greatly pleased with the sucess of her trick.

    A   B   C   D   N

Spelling - Exercise 8

The passage below contains some **spelling** errors. On each line, there is either **one** error or **no** error. Find the group of words containing the error and circle the corresponding letter beneath. **If there is no error, circle N.**

Celebrations in Barnford

1 Mayor Baxter has marked the begining of the week-long celebrations

A   B   C   D   N

2 for Barnford's centennial anniversery with the unveiling of a new

A   B   C   D   N

3 painting. Comissioned by the Mayor to commemorate 100 years

A   B   C   D   N

4 since Barnford was officially classifed as an industrial town, the piece

A   B   C   D   N

5 depicts the evolution of Barnford. It is currently exhibited at the

A   B   C   D   N

6 municipal building, but will shortly move to a new home in the gallary

A   B   C   D   N

7 of the recently renovated town museum. The curater, Maxwell Hardy,

A   B   C   D   N

8 said, "For a 100-year-old town, Barnford has such a rich history, which

A   B   C   D   N

the museum explores." It will be open to the public from the 1st of June.

Spelling - Exercise 9

The passage below contains some **spelling** errors. On each line, there is either **one** error or **no** error. Find the group of words containing the error and circle the corresponding letter beneath. **If there is no error, circle N.**

Dad's Secret Weapon

1 "No, I don't want to!" The wailing was to no avail; Jess's dad

A   B   C   D   N

2 merely scooped her up and deposeted her in the back seat. Her

A   B   C   D   N

3 mum's exasperated tone rang out harshly from the pasenger seat,

A   B   C   D   N

4 "Jessica, you're getting this injection or you're not coming on holiday."

A   B   C   D   N

5 But Jess's needle phobea trumped any desire to see giraffes in the wild.

A   B   C   D   N

6 "How about we grab some ice-cream afterwards? The tripel chocolate

A   B   C   D   N

7 sunday that you like." He'd said it, the magic words—the surly scowl

A   B   C   D   N

8 on Jess's face vanished and was immediately replaced with a smile.

A   B   C   D   N

Her parents chuckled; the 'good-cop, bad-cop' routine never failed.

Spelling - Exercise 10

The passage below contains some **spelling** errors. On each line, there is either **one** error or **no** error. Find the group of words containing the error and circle the corresponding letter beneath. **If there is no error, circle N.**

An extract from 'The Adventures of Tom Sawyer' by Mark Twain

1 Tom skirtled the block, and came round into a muddy alley that led by

    A   B   C   D   N

2 the back of his aunt's cow-stabel. He presently got safely beyond the

    A   B   C   D   N

3 reach of capture and punishment, and hastend toward the public

    A   B   C   D   N

4 square of the village, where two 'military' companys of boys had met

    A   B   C   D   N

5 for conflict, acording to previous appointment. Tom was General of

    A   B   C   D   N

6 one of these armys, Joe Harper (a bosom friend) General of the other.

    A   B   C   D   N

7 These two great commanders did not condesend to fight in person—

    A   B   C   D   N

8 that being better suited to the still smaller fry—but sat together on

    A   B   C   D   N

an eminence and conducted the field operation by orders delivered through aides-de-camps.

Spelling - Exercise 11

The passage below contains some **spelling** errors. On each line, there is either **one** error or **no** error. Find the group of words containing the error and circle the corresponding letter beneath. **If there is no error, circle N.**

An extract from 'Anne of Green Gables' by L.M. Montgomery

1 Anne felt that she could not have borne it if she had not been

A   B   C   D   N

2 going to the concert, for nothing else was disscussed that day

A   B   C   D   N

3 in school. The Avonlea Debateing Club, which met fortnightly all

A   B   C   D   N

4 winter, had had sevaral smaller free entertainments; but this

A   B   C   D   N

5 was to be a big affair, admission ten cents, in aid of the libary.

A   B   C   D   N

6 The Avonlea young people had been practiseing for weeks, and

A   B   C   D   N

7 all the scholars were especialy interested in it by reason of older

A   B   C   D   N

8 brothers and sisters who were going to take part.

A   B   C   D   N

Spelling - Exercise 12

The passage below contains some **spelling** errors. On each line, there is either **one** error or **no** error. Find the group of words containing the error and circle the corresponding letter beneath. **If there is no error, circle N.**

Jurassic Park

1 Based on the bestseller of the same name, Jurassic Park is a science-
    A   B   C   D   N

2 fiction franchise, centered around the survival attempts of humans
    A   B   C   D   N

3 following the escape of genetically-enginered dinosaurs. The concept
    A   B   C   D   N

4 was so popular that the film rights were bought even prier to the
    A   B   C   D   N

5 publication of the book. The enthuasiasm for the series continues
    A   B   C   D   N

6 with the fourth installment opening to a box-office record of $500
    A   B   C   D   N

7 million, despite being released over a decade after its predecesor. Its
    A   B   C   D   N

8 seqeul is already in the works with a scheduled release date of 2018.
    A   B   C   D   N

Spelling - Exercise 13

The sentences below contain some **spelling** errors. Each sentence has either **one** error or **no** error. Find the group of words containing the error and circle the corresponding letter beneath. **If there is no error, circle N.**

Sentences: Fiction

1 Laksi carefully placed the minuscle decorations on the cake's top tier.

A   B   C   D   N

2 The refferee was resolute in his decision not to award a penalty.

A   B   C   D   N

3 Kate's trip to Tanzania was an educational yet enjoyable experience.

A   B   C   D   N

4 The government ambassador always liased with the Foreign Office.

A   B   C   D   N

5 The children won't play near the cemetary as they believe it's haunted.

A   B   C   D   N

6 The adress looked vaguely familiar, but she couldn't remember why.

A   B   C   D   N

7 Determined to maintain his fitness, Jude followed a strict gym regieme.

A   B   C   D   N

8 Fortunately, Carl only suffered a minor concussion after the accident.

A   B   C   D   N

Spelling - Exercise 14

The passage below contains some **spelling** errors. On each line, there is either **one** error or **no** error. Find the group of words containing the error and circle the corresponding letter beneath. **If there is no error, circle N.**

An extract from 'Treasure Island' by Robert Louis Stevenson

1 Then all of a sudden there was a tremendous explotion of oaths

    A   B   C   D   N

2 and other noises—the chair and table went over in a lump, a

    A   B   C   D   N

3 clash of steele followed, and then a cry of pain, and the next

    A   B   C   D   N

4 instence I saw Black Dog in full flight, and the captain hotly

    A   B   C   D   N

5 pursueing, both with drawn cutlasses, and the former streaming

    A   B   C   D   N

6 blood from the left shoulder. Just at the door the captian aimed

    A   B   C   D   N

7 at the fugative one last tremendous cut, which would certainly

    A   B   C   D   N

8 have split him to the chin had it not been intercepeted by our big

    A   B   C   D   N

signboard of 'Admiral Benbow'.

Spelling - Exercise 15

The passage below contains some **spelling** errors. On each line, there is either **one** error or **no** error. Find the group of words containing the error and circle the corresponding letter beneath. **If there is no error, circle N.**

Motor Neurone Disease

1 Amyotrophic Lateral Sclerosis, more commonley known as Motor

A   B   C   D   N

2 Neurone Disease, is a progresive disorder where an individual's motor

A   B   C   D   N

3 neurons become damaged. The affects of this include an increasing

A   B   C   D   N

4 weakness in the mucsles and a visible reduction in their size, until the

A   B   C   D   N

5 body is eventually paralaysed. The condition is sometimes referred to

A   B   C   D   N

6 as Lou Gehrig's disease, named after the reputed American baseball

A   B   C   D   N

7 player who was diagnozed with the disease in 1939. It is also the

A   B   C   D   N

8 condition which affected the theoretical physicsist Stephen Hawking.

A   B   C   D   N

Punctuation

Punctuation - Exercise 1

The passage below contains some errors in the use of **punctuation**, including the use of **capital letters**. On each line, there is either **one** error or **no** error. Find the group of words containing the error and circle the corresponding letter beneath. **If there is no error, circle N.**

An extract from 'Through the Looking-Glass' by Lewis Carroll

1 It was not a very difficult question to answer, as there was only one road through the

   A   B   C   D   N

2 wood, and the two finger-posts both pointed along it. "I'll settle it" Alice said to herself,

   A   B   C   D   N

3 "when the road divides and they point different ways." but this did not seem likely to

   A   B   C   D   N

4 happen. She went on and on, a long way but wherever the road divided there were sure

   A   B   C   D   N

5 to be two finger-posts pointing the same way, one marked 'TO TWEEDLEDUMS HOUSE'

   A   B   C   D   N

6 and the other 'TO THE HOUSE OF TWEEDLEDEE' "I do believe," said Alice at last, "that

   A   B   C   D   N

7 they live in the same house! I wonder I never thought of that before—But I cant' stay

   A   B   C   D   N

8 there long. I'll just call and say 'how dyou do?' and ask them the way out of the wood."

   A   B   C   D   N

Punctuation - Exercise 2

The passage below contains some errors in the use of **punctuation**, including the use of **capital letters**. On each line, there is either **one** error or **no** error. Find the group of words containing the error and circle the corresponding letter beneath. **If there is no error, circle N.**

Hurricanes

1 depending on the ocean over which a tropical storm forms, it is given a different name:

    A   B   C   D   N

2 hurricane, if formed over the Atlantic or north-eastern Pacific Ocean; Cyclone, if formed

    A   B   C   D   N

3 over the South Pacific or Indian Ocean; and typhoon, if formed over the north-western

    A   B   C   D   N

4 Pacific. The strength of a hurricane is measured on the SaffirSimpson scale, which

    A   B   C   D   N

5 comprises five categories based on wind intensity. However this scale has been criticised

    A   B   C   D   N

6 for its' simplicity. Scientists find it difficult to predict the damage a hurricane will cause,

    A   B   C   D   N

7 although they have been trying for years. Regardless of the strength, of the hurricane,

    A   B   C   D   N

8 each storm has a low-pressure centre and strong winds that spiral round the out-side.

    A   B   C   D   N

Punctuation - Exercise 3

The passage below contains some errors in the use of **punctuation**, including the use of **capital letters**. On each line, there is either **one** error or **no** error. Find the group of words containing the error and circle the corresponding letter beneath. **If there is no error, circle N.**

An extract from 'The Emperor's New Clothes' by Hans Christian Andersen

1 many years ago, there was an Emperor, who was so excessively fond of new clothes,

  A   B   C   D   N

2 that he spent all his money in dress? He did not trouble himself in the least about his

  A   B   C   D   N

3 soldiers'; nor did he care to go either to the theatre or the chase, except for the

  A   B   C   D   N

4 opportunities then afforded him for displaying his new clothes. He had a different suit

  A   B   C   D   N

5 for each hour of the day; and as of any other king or emperor, One is accustomed to

  A   B   C   D   N

6 say, "He is sitting in council" it was always said of him, "The Emperor is sitting in his

  A   B   C   D   N

7 wardrobe. Time passed merrily in the large town which was his capital; strangers

  A   B   C   D   N

8 arrived every day at the court. One day, two rogues, calling themselves' weavers, made

  A   B   C   D   N

their appearance.

Punctuation - Exercise 4

The sentences below contain some errors in the use of **punctuation**, including the use of **capital letters**. Each sentence has either **one** error or **no** error. Find the group of words containing the error and circle the corresponding letter beneath. **If there is no error, circle N.**

Sentences from 'Pride and Prejudice' by Jane Austen

1 Mr. Bingley was good looking and gentleman-like he had a pleasant countenance.

　　　A　　　　B　　　　C　　　　D　　　　N

2 When they ascended the steps to the hall, Marias alarm was every moment increasing.

　　　A　　　　B　　　　C　　　　D　　　　N

3 As the weather was fine they had a pleasant walk of about half a mile across the park.

　　　A　　　　B　　　　C　　　　D　　　　N

4 I rather expected, from my knowledge of her affability, that it would happen.

　　　A　　　　B　　　　C　　　D　　　　N

5 I would not wish to be hasty in censuring anyone but I always speak what I think.

　　　A　　　　B　　　　C　　　　D　　　　N

6 Vanity and Pride are different things, though the words are often used synonymously.

　　　A　　　　B　　　　C　　　　D　　　　N

7 By nature friendly and obliging, his presentation at St. Jamess' had made him courteous.

　　　A　　　　B　　　　C　　　　D　　　　N

8 He never said a great deal, nor did she give, herself the trouble of listening much.

　　　A　　　　B　　　　C　　　　D　　　　N

Punctuation - Exercise 5

The passage below contains some errors in the use of **punctuation**, including the use of **capital letters**. On each line, there is either **one** error or **no** error. Find the group of words containing the error and circle the corresponding letter beneath. **If there is no error, circle N.**

An Old Treasure

1 The tattered and faded blanket had been in Lilys family for 19 years, since Tom, her

    A   B   C   D   N

2 brother had been born. It had journeyed around the world with them, from the snow-

    A   B   C   D   N

3 covered peaks of the Scottish Highlands to the sandy-shores of the south of Spain, and it

    A   B   C   D   N

4 wore the evidence of it's travels well. A faint patch of red was the only hint it had ever

    A   B   C   D   N

5 been anything other than its current greyish tinge. Everyone agreed, there was really no

    A   B   C   D   N

6 use for it now. it provided little protection from the cold, it was falling apart, and it even

    A   B   C   D   N

7 smelt musty. Yet no one had the heart to throw it away! It now lived up on the top shelf

    A   B   C   D   N

8 in Toms' bedroom, gathering dust and waiting to be rediscovered one day in the distant

    A   B   C   D   N

future.

Punctuation - Exercise 6

The passage below contains some errors in the use of **punctuation**, including the use of **capital letters**. On each line, there is either **one** error or **no** error. Find the group of words containing the error and circle the corresponding letter beneath. **If there is no error, circle N.**

Lacrosse

1 Well established by the 17th century the invention of lacrosse is attributed to the Native

A   B   C   D   N

2 Americans. Although it is one of the oldest team sport's in North America, its name is

A   B   C   D   N

3 derived from a French word, 'la crosse, which aptly translates as 'the stick'. Despite its

A   B   C   D   N

4 origins, the modern-style of lacrosse played today is a modified form created by

A   B   C   D   N

5 European immigrants. There now exist four differing forms of the game, but the

A   B   C   D   N

6 fundamental aim of the game remains the same: players must cradle pass and shoot the

A   B   C   D   N

7 ball into the opposite teams goal to score. Lacrosse has not been included in the

A   B   C   D   N

8 olympics since 1948, when it was only a demonstration sport. Efforts to reinstate it as an

A   B   C   D   N

Olympic medal sport are ongoing.

Punctuation - Exercise 7

The sentences below contain some errors in the use of **punctuation**, including the use of **capital letters**. Each sentence has either **one** error or **no** error. Find the group of words containing the error and circle the corresponding letter beneath. **If there is no error, circle N.**

Sentences: Fiction

1 In order to make a meringue, you need egg whites, beaten; sugar; and cream optional.

    A   B   C   D   N

2 "Lets go! The play's meant to start at seven o'clock," called Tim, running ahead of Dad.

    A   B   C   D   N

3 Do you think your fearless? Find out this Friday at Fright Night for only £10 per person!

    A   B   C   D   N

4 "Can you do some work please" exclaimed Niki to Damian, who rolled his eyes in reply.

    A   B   C   D   N

5 I'm going to Seville, Spain; Athens Greece; Istanbul, Turkey; and Dublin, Ireland.

    A   B   C   D   N

6 The park has one hundred-year-old trees, which I helped plant last May with my class.

    A   B   C   D   N

7 Lakgana devoured a pear, several cookies and a cake: she hadnt eaten all day long.

    A   B   C   D   N

8 "My mum's going to kill me" cried Helen. "This stain will never come out of the shirt!"

    A   B   C   D   N

Punctuation - Exercise 8

The passage below contains some errors in the use of **punctuation**, including the use of **capital letters**. On each line, there is either **one** error or **no** error. Find the group of words containing the error and circle the corresponding letter beneath. **If there is no error, circle N.**

Dear Diary

1 There are only ten days left before Christmas! I keep trying to hint to Mum that I would
   A   B   C   D   N

2 love a new bike but she doesn't seem to have noticed. She can be so oblivious at times.
   A   B   C   D   N

3 Kevin my oldest friend, still thinks it's Father Christmas who brings all the presents, and
   A   B   C   D   N

4 he didn't believe me when I said it was our parents, so now were not talking to each
   A   B   C   D   N

5 other. I think I'll make up with him on Monday; its really annoying playing Peter Pan
   A   B   C   D   N

6 without a Captain Hook. Tomorrow, we're going to the ice skating rink for the twin's
   A   B   C   D   N

7 birthdays. Should I invite Kevin to join us! I think he'd like that. I really hope the twins
   A   B   C   D   N

8 like their birthday presents: it took me ages to pick out the right colour watch strap for
   A   B   C   D   N

each of them!   Gemma

Punctuation - Exercise 9

The passage below contains some errors in the use of **punctuation**, including the use of **capital letters**. On each line, there is either **one** error or **no** error. Find the group of words containing the error and circle the corresponding letter beneath. **If there is no error, circle N.**

An extract from 'White Fang' by Jack London

1
Leather harnesses were on the dogs, and leather traces' attached them to a sled which

A   B   C   D   N

2
dragged along behind. The sled was without runners. It was made of stout, birch-bark

A   B   C   D   N

3
and it's full surface rested on the snow. The front end of the sled was turned up, like a

A   B   C   D   N

4
scroll, in order to force down and under the bore of soft-snow that surged like a wave

A   B   C   D   N

5
before it. On the sled, securely lashed was a long and narrow oblong box. There were

A   B   C   D   N

6
other things on the sled—blankets, an axe, and a coffee-pot and Frying-pan; but

A   B   C   D   N

7
prominent, occupying most of the space, was the long, and narrow oblong box. In

A   B   C   D   N

8
advance of the dogs, on wide snowshoes, toiled a man. At the rear of the sled toiled a

A   B   C   D   N

second man.

Punctuation - Exercise 10

The passage below contains some errors in the use of **punctuation**, including the use of **capital letters**. On each line, there is either **one** error or **no** error. Find the group of words containing the error and circle the corresponding letter beneath. **If there is no error, circle N.**

Waiting

1 I waited with bated breath the coarse bark digging into my back, but the momentary

    A   B   C   D   N

2 discomfort was made bearable by the knowledge that here I would'nt be found. He

    A   B   C   D   N

3 couldn't have followed me I had been checking back every so often to make sure he

    A   B   C   D   N

4 hadn't. I started breathing deeply and steadily in an attempt to calm myself down,

    A   B   C   D   N

5 focusing on the air flowing in through my nose and rushing out through my mouth The

    A   B   C   D   N

6 paranoia had been kicking in over the past, few minutes; the silence, once so

    A   B   C   D   N

7 comforting, was now unnerving. What was that? Oh, it was just a squirrel. With a sigh of

    A   B   C   D   N

8 relief I slumped against the tree when, 'Found you!' came a gleeful cry. Why did I always

    A   B   C   D   N

lose at hide-and-seek?

Punctuation - Exercise 11

The passage below contains some errors in the use of **punctuation**, including the use of **capital letters**. On each line, there is either **one** error or **no** error. Find the group of words containing the error and circle the corresponding letter beneath. **If there is no error, circle N.**

An extract from 'The Story of Doctor Doolittle' by Hugh Lofting

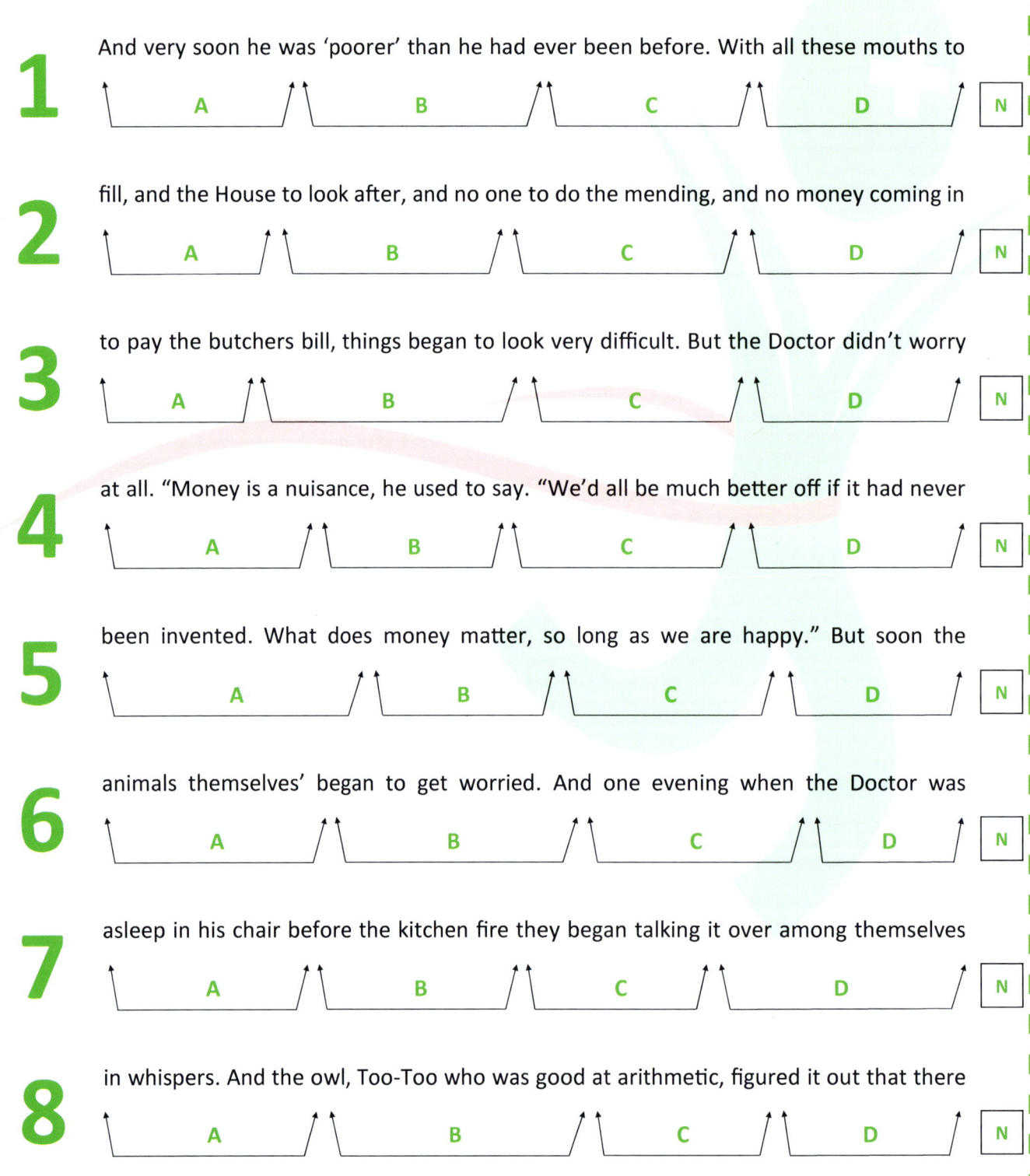

1. And very soon he was 'poorer' than he had ever been before. With all these mouths to
   A   B   C   D   N

2. fill, and the House to look after, and no one to do the mending, and no money coming in
   A   B   C   D   N

3. to pay the butchers bill, things began to look very difficult. But the Doctor didn't worry
   A   B   C   D   N

4. at all. "Money is a nuisance, he used to say. "We'd all be much better off if it had never
   A   B   C   D   N

5. been invented. What does money matter, so long as we are happy." But soon the
   A   B   C   D   N

6. animals themselves' began to get worried. And one evening when the Doctor was
   A   B   C   D   N

7. asleep in his chair before the kitchen fire they began talking it over among themselves
   A   B   C   D   N

8. in whispers. And the owl, Too-Too who was good at arithmetic, figured it out that there
   A   B   C   D   N

was only money enough left to last another week.

Punctuation - Exercise 12

The passage below contains some errors in the use of **punctuation**, including the use of **capital letters**. On each line, there is either **one** error or **no** error. Find the group of words containing the error and circle the corresponding letter beneath. **If there is no error, circle N.**

Muhammad Ali

1 Float like a butterfly, sting like a bee.' Does that sound familiar? Not just a professional

A   B   C   D   N

2 boxer but also a pioneering activist, Muhammad Alis' tongue was just as fast as his

A   B   C   D   N

3 footwork. Following his gold-medal win, at the 1960s Olympics, his boxing career

A   B   C   D   N

4 flourished culminating in his title as the world heavyweight champion. In fact, he

A   B   C   D   N

5 remains the only boxer to have earned this Title three times. Yet it was his work outside

A   B   C   D   N

6 of the ring, which earned him the Presidential Medal of Freedom; he was a passionate

A   B   C   D   N

7 advocate for civil rights, and did much to support the African American community in

A   B   C   D   N

8 the USA. However, even the Peoples Champion's fight had to come to an end, as it did in

A   B   C   D   N

2016 after his lengthy battle with Parkinson's disease.

Punctuation - Exercise 13

The sentences below contain some errors in the use of **punctuation**, including the use of **capital letters**. Each sentence has either **one** error or **no** error. Find the group of words containing the error and circle the corresponding letter beneath. **If there is no error, circle N.**

Sentences: Non-Fiction

1 An orchestra comprises strings, woodwind percussion and brass, and often a piano.

A   B   C   D   N

2 Did you know Britain was connected to France, by land until around 10,000 years ago?

A   B   C   D   N

3 The *Harry Potter* series has been translated into 74 languages, including Ancient greek!

A   B   C   D   N

4 Your born with about 270 individual bones, but by adulthood you only have 206.

A   B   C   D   N

5 Teddy bears are named after a former US President who was commonly called Teddy'.

A   B   C   D   N

6 Renaissance artist Michelangelo was also a prolific sculptor, poet and architect.

A   B   C   D   N

7 The worlds fastest animal is the peregrine falcon, which can travel at up to 389 km/h.

A   B   C   D   N

8 The Hundred Years' War in fact lasted for 116 years and was waged, from 1337 to 1453.

A   B   C   D   N

Punctuation - Exercise 14

The passage below contains some errors in the use of **punctuation**, including the use of **capital letters**. On each line, there is either **one** error or **no** error. Find the group of words containing the error and circle the corresponding letter beneath. **If there is no error, circle N.**

Overcooked

1 Peter anxiously surveyed the gathering, keeping an eye out for any trouble. He knew he

　A　　　　　B　　　　　C　　　　　D　　　N

2 shouldnt have such low opinions of his own relatives, but after last year's get-together,

　A　　　　　B　　　　　C　　　　　D　　　N

3 he wasn't taking any chances. Oh dear, Why was Granny Beatrice nattering to Uncle

　A　　　　　B　　　　　C　　　　　D　　　N

4 Eddie? Conversations between those two never ended well! Abandoning the barbecue,

　A　　　　　B　　　　　C　　　　　D　　　N

5 he hastily went to steer her in the direction of, his cousin Samantha. She was a much

　A　　　　　B　　　　　C　　　　　D　　　N

6 safer option. Suddenly, the acrid stench of charred remains stopped him, in his tracks. "I

　A　　　　　B　　　　　C　　　　　D　　　N

7 think it will have to be pizza instead," he groaned as his family chuckled Oh well, at least

　A　　　　　B　　　　　C　　　　　D　　　N

8 this year it was just burnt hot dogs and not broken bones? Peter decided to class that as

　A　　　　　B　　　　　C　　　　　D　　　N

an improvement.

Punctuation - Exercise 15

The passage below contains some errors in the use of **punctuation**, including the use of **capital letters**. On each line, there is either **one** error or **no** error. Find the group of words containing the error and circle the corresponding letter beneath. **If there is no error, circle N.**

RMS *Titanic*

1 When you hear the word 'Titanic', what do you think of. If the critically acclaimed film

A   B   C   D   N

2 starring Leonardo DiCaprio and Kate Winslet came to mind, then your'e not in the

A   B   C   D   N

3 minority. The Academy Award-winning film is based on the journey of RMS *Titanic*, a

A   B   C   D   N

4 luxury passenger liner; infamous worldwide for having sunk on her maiden voyage from

A   B   C   D   N

5 Southampton to New York in 1912. constructed in Belfast, *Titanic* was the largest ship

A   B   C   D   N

6 afloat at her time (of service), and it was generally believed that ice posed no danger to

A   B   C   D   N

7 large vessels such as herself. However, at 11.40pm on the 14th April 1912, she hit an

A   B   C   D   N

8 iceberg off the south coast of Newfoundland. Water breached five-of-her-sixteen

A   B   C   D   N

watertight compartments and she sank 2 hours and 40 minutes later.

FIRST PAST THE POST®

Grammar & Word Choice

Grammar & Word Choice - Exercise 1

For each question, choose the most appropriate word or group of words so that the passage below makes sense. Only **one** of the five answers is correct. Circle the corresponding letter beneath.

Backgammon

Popularised

1

nowhere	locally	nationwide	globally	generally
A	B	C	D	E

in the late 20th century, backgammon is one of the world's oldest board games.

2

Whereas	When	Whilst	Without	Where
A	B	C	D	E

the exact origins are unknown, it is

3

expect	believed	accept	belief	believe
A	B	C	D	E

to be a direct descendant of the Greek board game, 'Tabula'. Backgammon is a two-player game that

4

involves	involve	involved	involving	invoking
A	B	C	D	E

rolling a pair of dice and moving one's counters

5

surrounding	around	among	next to	alongside
A	B	C	D	E

the board. The aim of the game is for the individual to

6

attach	place	connect	remove	win
A	B	C	D	E

all their pieces from the board

7

whilst	when	if	as long as	before
A	B	C	D	E

their opponent does. Success in the game is

8

relies	dependent	determine	independent	established
A	B	C	D	E

on not only skill but also an element of luck.

Grammar & Word Choice - Exercise 2

For each question, choose the most appropriate word or group of words so that the passage below makes sense. Only **one** of the five answers is correct. Circle the corresponding letter beneath.

Tricky Trailers

1 For how much Sally loved going to the cinema, she absolutely

loved	preferred	loathed	appreciated	shunned
A	B	C	D	E

2 the trailers that ran before the film. She was sure that they were

uselessly	persistently	necessarily	delightfully	deliberately
A	B	C	D	E

3 long so that cinema-goers would finish their popcorn

during	after	before	between	if
A	B	C	D	E

4 the film started and be forced into buying more. The price of popcorn

are	were	was	is	will be
A	B	C	D	E

5 already extortionate and she was determined not to

keep up	lay	avoid	set	fall into
A	B	C	D	E

6 that trap again. That's why she decided this time she was going

delaying	delays	delayed	to delay	for delays
A	B	C	D	E

7 going into the cinema until just before the film started.

Dismally,	Thankfully,	Funnily,	Unluckily,	Luckily,
A	B	C	D	E

8 she chose the one day when the trailers

streamed	stopped	paused	skipped	replayed
A	B	C	D	E

early, and she ended up missing the first half hour of the film!

Grammar & Word Choice - Exercise 3

For each question, choose the most appropriate word or group of words so that the passage below makes sense. Only **one** of the five answers is correct. Circle the corresponding letter beneath.

An extract from 'The Wind in the Willows' by Kenneth Grahame

The Mole had to be

1

satiate	satisfy	content	contend	please
A	B	C	D	E

with this. But the Badger never came along and every day

2

brang	bought	bring	brought	brung
A	B	C	D	E

its amusements, and it was not till

3

days	summer	months	season	winter
A	B	C	D	E

was long over, and cold and frost and miry ways kept

4

us	their	all	they	them
A	B	C	D	E

much indoors and the swollen river raced past

5

outdoors	within	inside	indoors	outside
A	B	C	D	E

their windows with a speed that mocked at boating of any sort or kind, that he

6

think	heard	found	thought	find
A	B	C	D	E

his thoughts dwelling again with

7

less	little	most	much	many
A	B	C	D	E

persistence on the solitary grey Badger, who lived his own life

8

on	by	from	as	with
A	B	C	D	E

himself, in his hole in the middle of the Wild Wood.

Grammar & Word Choice - Exercise 4

For each question, choose the most appropriate word or group of words so that the passage below makes sense. Only **one** of the five answers is correct. Circle the corresponding letter beneath.

Trams

1 Trams are public transportation vehicles

whose	which were	those	who	that
A	B	C	D	E

2 run on tracks laid out on public streets. A network of

temporary	an individual	established	no	much
A	B	C	D	E

3 trams forms a tramway, and

their	these	this	it	them
A	B	C	D	E

4 travel through cities, towns and even between countries.

With	Regardless	Even though	Despite	Because of
A	B	C	D	E

5 continued investment into developing tram systems, when

connected	coordinated	compared	converted	confirmed
A	B	C	D	E

6 to buses and automobiles, certain countries still

disregard	thinking	consider	doubt	viewing
A	B	C	D	E

7 them cumbersome, dangerous and ineffective. However, in central and eastern Europe, the infrastructure

are been	has been	had been	will be	are not
A	B	C	D	E

8 refined and they are rewarded with a fast, flexible and energy-

effective	effort	effect	efficient	effable
A	B	C	D	E

mode of transport.

Grammar & Word Choice - Exercise 5

For each question, choose the most appropriate word or group of words so that the passage below makes sense. Only **one** of the five answers is correct. Circle the corresponding letter beneath.

Piled-Up Paperwork

Harold groaned in

1

happiness	fear	despair	excitement	anger
A	B	C	D	E

at the sight of all the paperwork that had built

2

along	across	down	up	over
A	B	C	D	E

on his desk over the past few days. This was why he

3

scarce	often	always	never	hardly
A	B	C	D	E

ever went on holiday; his colleagues always said they could

4

look over	hold up	handle	care for	appreciate
A	B	C	D	E

the office without him, but then this happened. This time

5

tomorrow	today	yesterday	last year	next month
A	B	C	D	E

he had been

6

laying	lying	laid up	lie down	lied
A	B	C	D	E

on a sandy beach in the middle of the Maldives. What a difference a day made! Peering down at his

7

watch,	organiser,	calendar,	alarm,	journal,
A	B	C	D	E

he gave a resigned sigh; only three months until his

8

last	final	next	immediate	future
A	B	C	D	E

holiday.

Grammar & Word Choice - Exercise 6

For each question, choose the most appropriate word or group of words so that the passage below makes sense. Only **one** of the five answers is correct. Circle the corresponding letter beneath.

Dear Uncle Bernard

Thank you so much for the card and money you

1

send me	sent to I	sent me	sending me	sended me
A	B	C	D	E

for my birthday last week.

2

I am	I have	I will	I has	I would
A	B	C	D	E

been saving up so I can buy the latest FIFA game, and your gift means I

3

can	should	can not	might not	ought
A	B	C	D	E

be able to buy it by the end of June! I've asked Dad to give me more chores

4

however	since	because	so	and
A	B	C	D	E

I can earn a little extra money, but I

5

can refuse	will refuse	refuses	refuse	refusing
A	B	C	D	E

to throw the bins out; they're too smelly! I was really upset that

6

I	we	he	your	you
A	B	C	D	E

couldn't come to my birthday party, but Auntie Ellen said you're busy

7

around	over	on	at	in
A	B	C	D	E

Egypt, digging up fossils. Do you think you'll be back in time for Christmas?

8

Many	Little	Lots of	A lot of	Lot of
A	B	C	D	E

love,

Your favourite nephew

For each question, choose the most appropriate word or group of words so that the passage below makes sense. Only **one** of the five answers is correct. Circle the corresponding letter beneath.

An extract from 'The Elves and the Shoemaker' by The Brothers Grimm

His conscience was clear and his heart light

1

by	amidst	away	over	along
A	B	C	D	E

all his troubles; so he went peaceably to bed, left all his

2

thinking	worry	fear	cares	emotions
A	B	C	D	E

to Heaven, and soon fell asleep. In the

3

morning	dusk	afternoon	night	daylight
A	B	C	D	E

after he had said his prayers, he sat himself down to his work; when, to his great wonder, there

4

still	stand	stood	fell	fall
A	B	C	D	E

the shoes all ready made,

5

outside	across	within	upon	besides
A	B	C	D	E

the table. The good man knew not what to say or think at such an

6

expected	odd	bizarre	regular	anticipated
A	B	C	D	E

thing happening. He looked at the workmanship; there was

7

none	not	no	neither	nil
A	B	C	D	E

one false stitch in the whole job; all was so

8

organise	untidy	false	strayed	neat
A	B	C	D	E

and true, that it was quite a masterpiece.

Grammar & Word Choice - Exercise 8

For each question, choose the most appropriate word or group of words so that the passage below makes sense. Only **one** of the five answers is correct. Circle the corresponding letter beneath.

The NHS

The National Health Service (NHS) is the healthcare system currently

1

using	trialled	founded	operating	works
A	B	C	D	E

in England. When first introduced in 1948, the NHS was built upon three

2

final	foundation	temporary	peripheral	fundamental
A	B	C	D	E

principles: that it was available for all, that it

3

were freed	is free	was free	were free	was freed
A	B	C	D	E

at the point of use, and that it met everybody's needs. Although these principles remain

4

in the same	on	in	at the	within its
A	B	C	D	E

place, the NHS has found itself under significant

5

benefits	reward	cost	weight	pressure
A	B	C	D	E

in recent years. With an ageing population, an

6

fall	increase	rise	decrease	expansion
A	B	C	D	E

in chronic health conditions and staff shortages, it is clear that its services

7

will be	were	can be	is	are
A	B	C	D	E

overstretched. As spending on healthcare

8

slowing	slows	slowed	slow	are slowing
A	B	C	D	E

down year on year, there are worries about the future of the NHS.

Grammar & Word Choice - Exercise 9

For each question, choose the most appropriate word or group of words so that the sentences below make sense. Only **one** of the five answers is correct. Circle the corresponding letter beneath.

Sentences: Fiction

1 There was

anything	nothing	something	a thing	everything
A	B	C	D	E

on the table when we left this morning, so where did it all come from?

2 She couldn't go to the concert; all the tickets

will sell	could sell	had sold	have sold	are selling
A	B	C	D	E

out the week before.

3 Her parents only allow her to play video games after she

finish	has finished	can finish	had finished	finishing
A	B	C	D	E

all her homework.

4

Wherever	Although	Even as	Since	When
A	B	C	D	E

she fell off her bike, she has started wearing protective gear.

5

"Whose	"Whos	"Who's	"Whom is	"What is
A	B	C	D	E

that player in the red shirt?" asked the scout. "He's got potential."

6 Yasmin couldn't commit to chess club as it

concurred	conceded	conflicted	coordinated	collaborated
A	B	C	D	E

with her basketball practice.

7 The ball soared

around	over	on	at	through
A	B	C	D	E

the wooden fence and into next door's garden.

8 There were too

much	little	lots of	small	few
A	B	C	D	E

students there to make the lesson worthwhile.

Grammar & Word Choice - Exercise 10

For each question, choose the most appropriate word or group of words so that the passage below makes sense. Only **one** of the five answers is correct. Circle the corresponding letter beneath.

An extract from 'A Christmas Carol' by Charles Dickens

Oh! But he was a tight-fisted hand

1

as	in	at	for	of
A	B	C	D	E

the grindstone, Scrooge! A squeezing, wrenching, grasping, scraping, clutching,

2

guilty	benevolent	covert	covetous	courteous
A	B	C	D	E

old sinner! Hard and sharp as flint, from

3

where	which	what	whom	that
A	B	C	D	E

no steel had ever struck out generous fire;

4

secrete	secretively	secrecy	secrets	secret
A	B	C	D	E

and self-contained,

5

nor	but	so	yet	and
A	B	C	D	E

solitary as an oyster. The cold within him

6

frozen	freezed	freeze	froze	freezing
A	B	C	D	E

his old features, nipped his pointed nose, shrivelled his cheek, stiffened his gait;

7

got	get	make	making	made
A	B	C	D	E

his eyes red, his thin lips blue; and

8

speaking	spoken	spoke	speak	say
A	B	C	D	E

out shrewdly in his grating voice.

Grammar & Word Choice - Exercise 11

For each question, choose the most appropriate word or group of words so that the passage below makes sense. Only **one** of the five answers is correct. Circle the corresponding letter beneath.

Google

1 Google Inc. is a multi-national

businesses	corporate	branding	company	office
A	B	C	D	E

2 most well-known for its international search engine. Since its

created	creating	creation	creates	create
A	B	C	D	E

3 in 1998 by two university students, the company has expanded to

provision	offer	demand	increase	serve
A	B	C	D	E

4 more than 50 internet services, including e-mail, books and maps,

in addition	in spite of	during	as well as	at the same
A	B	C	D	E

5 the mobile operating system, Android. It is

able	skilled at	capable	possible	apt
A	B	C	D	E

6 of handling over a billion search requests per day which requires

utilising	promoting	writing	reading	analysing
A	B	C	D	E

7 millions of pages a second. The founders were

accepted	willing	unsure	forced	reluctant
A	B	C	D	E

8 to sell it for $1 million in 1999 but were rejected; it is now the world's

overpriced	least	estimated	most	highest
A	B	C	D	E

valuable brand, worth over $100 billion.

Grammar & Word Choice - Exercise 12

For each question, choose the most appropriate word or group of words so that the sentences below make sense. Only **one** of the five answers is correct. Circle the corresponding letter beneath.

Sentences: Non-Fiction

1 The pavlova, a meringue-based cake, is

name	names	to be named	named	naming
A	B	C	D	E

after the Russian ballerina, Anna Pavlovna Pavlova.

2 Wimbledon is the oldest and

many	most	very	even	little
A	B	C	D	E

prestigious tennis tournament in the world.

3 The well-known playwright, William Shakespeare,

producing	producer	produces	is producing	produced
A	B	C	D	E

a plethora of plays and sonnets during his lifetime.

4 The moon landing is

always	widely	unusually	least	few
A	B	C	D	E

regarded as NASA's greatest achievement.

5 The model who posed for Leonardo da Vinci's the *Mona Lisa*

remains	is remaining	remainer	remain	remaining
A	B	C	D	E

a great mystery.

6 Boudica was a Celtic queen,

for who	who	for whom	whoever	whomever
A	B	C	D	E

the Romans were the greatest enemy.

7 The Harry Potter books have been translated

for	to	onto	in	into
A	B	C	D	E

75 languages over the past two decades.

8 After an exhausting voyage

lasts	lasted	lasting	had lasting	has lasted
A	B	C	D	E

1,742 days, the naturalist Charles Darwin finally returned to England.

Grammar & Word Choice - Exercise 13

For each question, choose the most appropriate word or group of words so that the passage below makes sense. Only **one** of the five answers is correct. Circle the corresponding letter beneath.

An extract from 'The Secret Garden' by Frances Hodgson Burnett

It was the sweetest, most mysterious-looking place any one could

1

see.	dream.	neglect.	think.	imagine.
A	B	C	D	E

The high walls which shut it in were

2

cover	covering	covered	covers	to cover
A	B	C	D	E

with the leafless stems of climbing roses which were so thick they were

3

twist	separated	ordered	matted	intimate
A	B	C	D	E

together. Mary Lennox knew they were roses

4

although	however	therefore	despite	because
A	B	C	D	E

she had seen a great many roses in India. All the

5

floors	ground	everything	road	sky
A	B	C	D	E

was covered with grass of a wintry brown and out of it grew

6

chunk	single	clumps	individual	roots
A	B	C	D	E

of bushes which were

7

neither	surely	doubtfully	maybe	certain
A	B	C	D	E

rose-bushes if they

8

was	were	are	were not	be
A	B	C	D	E

alive.

Grammar & Word Choice - Exercise 14

For each question, choose the most appropriate word or group of words so that the passage below makes sense. Only **one** of the five answers is correct. Circle the corresponding letter beneath.

The Great Wall of China

Built along the northern borders of China, the

1

construction	fabrication	built	demolition	ruins
A	B	C	D	E

of the Great Wall dates as far back as the 7th century. Although

2

never	rarely	seldom	commonly	occasional
A	B	C	D	E

mistaken as one long wall, the Great Wall does in fact

3

comprising	comprised	comprise	to comprise	comprises
A	B	C	D	E

several walls, built by

4

succeeding	successive	successful	succulent	succumbing
A	B	C	D	E

dynasties. In 1987, it was designated a UNESCO World Heritage Site, however remnants of

5

it's	it is	its	it was	it
A	B	C	D	E

previous function as a

6

fight	battle	attack	protect	defence
A	B	C	D	E

mechanism are still present. Dotted

7

over	above	along	long	around
A	B	C	D	E

the wall are watchtowers and fortresses, once used for surveillance

8

with	by	between	against	behind
A	B	C	D	E

invasions, now an enduring symbol of China's prowess.

Grammar & Word Choice - Exercise 15

For each question, choose the most appropriate word or group of words so that the passage below makes sense. Only **one** of the five answers is correct. Circle the corresponding letter beneath.

An extract from 'Tarzan of the Apes' by Edgar Rice Burroughs

Not thirty paces behind the

1

both	twice	to	two	too
A	B	C	D	E

she crouched—Sabor, the huge lioness—lashing her tail.

2

Joyfully	Gracelessly	Rapidly	Secretively	Cautiously
A	B	C	D	E

she moved a great padded paw

3

front,	forward,	backwards,	behind,	upward,
A	B	C	D	E

noiselessly placing it before she lifted the next. Thus she advanced;

4

hers	she	her	herself	its
A	B	C	D	E

belly low, almost touching the

5

ceiling	edge	base	surface	core
A	B	C	D	E

of the ground—a great cat preparing to

6

sprang	spring	springing	sprung	springs
A	B	C	D	E

upon its prey. Now she was

7

in	with in	with	close	within
A	B	C	D	E

ten feet of the two unsuspecting little playfellows —carefully she

8

drew	drawn	drawing	draw	was drawn
A	B	C	D	E

her hind feet well up beneath her body, great muscles rolling under the beautiful skin.

Mixed Test 1

12 minutes

Marking Grid																								Total
Spelling								Punctuation								Grammar & Word Choice								
1	2	3	4	5	6	7	8	9	10	11	12	13	14	15	16	17	18	19	20	21	22	23	24	
																								/24

Mixed Test 1 - Spelling

4 minutes

The passage below contains some **spelling** errors. On each line, there is either **one** error or **no** error. Find the group of words containing the error and circle the corresponding letter beneath. **If there is no error, circle N.**

An extract from 'Heidi' by Johanna Spyri

1   The children in the meantime were asending slowly in a zigzag
       A   B   C   D   N

2   way, Peter always knowing were to find all sorts of good
          A   B   C   D   N

3   grasing places for his goats where they could nibble. Thus they
          A   B   C   D   N

4   strayed from side to side. The poor little girl had folowed the
          A   B   C   D   N

5   boy with only the greatest effort and she was panting in her
          A   B   C   D   N

6   heavy clothes. She was so hot and uncomfortible that she only
          A   B   C   D   N

7   climbed by exerting all her strenth. She did not say anything
          A   B   C   D   N

8   but looked envyously at Peter, who jumped about so easily.
          A   B   C   D   N

Mixed Test 1 - Punctuation

 **4 minutes**

The passage below contains some errors in the use of **punctuation**, including the use of **capital letters**. On each line, there is either **one** error or **no** error. Find the group of words containing the error and circle the corresponding letter beneath. **If there is no error, circle N.**

My Time Had Come

1 A smattering of applause signalled that my time, was up. Months of practice had boiled

    A   B   C   D   N

2 down to this. "don't look straight ahead, don't stand too close to the mic, and don't

    A   B   C   D   N

3 forget to smile!" Mums voice was echoing in my head. The first few beats of the familiar

    A   B   C   D   N

4 introduction filled the auditorium. Taking a deep, breath, I opened my mouth... but

    A   B   C   D   N

5 nothing came out! I could feel my throat closing-up and hot tears beginning to form.

    A   B   C   D   N

6 Desperately, I tried again my second attempt was more successful. A few notes warbled

    A   B   C   D   N

7 out; they didn't sound anything like what Id practiced, but they were better than

    A   B   C   D   N

8 nothing! Growing in confidence, I pressed on and, before I knew it, I'd reached the end

    A   B   C   D   N

of the song, and the audience had leapt to their feet.

 **4 minutes**

For each question, choose the most appropriate word or group of words so that the passage below makes sense. Only **one** of the five answers is correct. Circle the corresponding letter beneath.

Pokémon

1 When Satoshi Tajiri designed Pokémon in 1995, it is

probable	definite	unlikely	impossible	potential
A	B	C	D	E

2 that he anticipated just how popular the fictional creatures

have been.	would be.	could be.	are to be.	can not be.
A	B	C	D	E

3 A portmanteau for 'pocket monsters', the Pokémon media

work	franchise	craze	group	product
A	B	C	D	E

4 now spans not only the original video games,

as well as	yet	but	with	in
A	B	C	D	E

5 also trading card games, animated series, and most

lately,	recently,	often,	frequently,	new,
A	B	C	D	E

6 a mobile, augmented-reality game. Despite the evolution in

modes	method	way	how	games
A	B	C	D	E

7 of play, the concept remains the

equivalent,	same,	similar,	identical,	exact,
A	B	C	D	E

8 Pokémon trainers must catch and train

your	his	their	her	our
A	B	C	D	E

Pokémon in battle.

52

Mixed Test 2

 12 minutes

Marking Grid																								Total
Punctuation								Grammar & Word Choice								Spelling								
1	2	3	4	5	6	7	8	9	10	11	12	13	14	15	16	17	18	19	20	21	22	23	24	
																								/24

4 minutes

The passage below contains some errors in the use of **punctuation**, including the use of **capital letters**. On each line, there is either **one** error or **no** error. Find the group of words containing the error and circle the corresponding letter beneath. **If there is no error, circle N.**

An extract from 'The Prince and the Pauper' by Mark Twain

1 Toms breath came quick and short with excitement, and his eyes grew big with wonder

A   B   C   D   N

2 and delight everything gave way in his mind instantly to one desire: that was to get

A   B   C   D   N

3 close to the prince, and have a good devouring look at him. Before he knew what he

A   B   C   D   N

4 was about, he had his face against the gate-bars. the next instant one of the soldiers

A   B   C   D   N

5 snatched him rudely away, and sent him spinning among the gaping crowd of country

A   B   C   D   N

6 gawks and london idlers. The soldier said, "Mind thy manners, thou young beggar!" The

A   B   C   D   N

7 crowd jeered and laughed; but the young Prince sprang to the gate with his face

A   B   C   D   N

8 flushed, and his eyes flashing with indignation, and cried out, "how dar'st though use a

A   B   C   D   N

poor lad like that?"

Mixed Test 2 - Grammar & Word Choice

 **4 minutes**

For each question, choose the most appropriate word or group of words so that the passage below makes sense. Only **one** of the five answers is correct. Circle the corresponding letter beneath.

Lost!

A large black Labrador

1

by	with	at	for	upon
A	B	C	D	E

noticeable white streaks on her ears. She was

2

next seen	last saw	first seen	first saw	last seen
A	B	C	D	E

in State Park, wearing a turquoise collar inscribed with

3

a	an	the	its	his
A	B	C	D	E

'H'. She responds to the name 'Holly' and may

4

be carrying	carrying	carried	carries	will carry
A	B	C	D	E

a red spotted ball. There is a reward

5

onto	on	out of	off	of
A	B	C	D	E

£200 available for anyone who finds her and a

6

free	better	worse	larger	smaller
A	B	C	D	E

sum of £50 for anyone who can provide information on her whereabouts.

7

When	If	Where	Whatever	However
A	B	C	D	E

found, please call us on 01234567890 or

8

bottle	leave	take	prepare	read
A	B	C	D	E

a text message.

 **4 minutes**

The passage below contains some **spelling** errors. On each line, there is either **one** error or **no** error. Find the group of words containing the error and circle the corresponding letter beneath. **If there is no error, circle N.**

Global Warming

1 Global warming is the gradual increase in the averege temperature

    A   B   C   D   N

2 of the Earth's atmasphere. Despite the temperature increasing

    A   B   C   D   N

3 naturelly as a result of geological cycles, in recent years, it has been

    A   B   C   D   N

4 acelerating at an unprecedented rate. Scientists have shown this is a

    A   B   C   D   N

5 result of the increased emission of carbon dioxede and other

    A   B   C   D   N

6 greenhouse gases, causing the atmosphere to trap more heat, making

    A   B   C   D   N

7 the planet warmer. The disastrous effects of this can be seen as

    A   B   C   D   N

8 rising sea levels, melting ice caps and increasing dessert expansion.

    A   B   C   D   N

Mixed Test 3

12 minutes

Marking Grid																								Total
Grammar & Word Choice								Spelling								Punctuation								
1	2	3	4	5	6	7	8	9	10	11	12	13	14	15	16	17	18	19	20	21	22	23	24	
																								/24

Mixed Test 3 - Grammar & Word Choice

 4 minutes

For each question, choose the most appropriate word or group of words so that the passage below makes sense. Only **one** of the five answers is correct. Circle the corresponding letter beneath.

An extract from 'Robinson Crusoe' by Daniel Defoe

But as soon as it

1

grows	growing	grow	grown	grew
A	B	C	D	E

dusk in the evening, I changed my course,

2

for	and	as	yet	plus
A	B	C	D	E

steered directly south and by east, bending my course a little towards the east, that I might

3

keep	kept	be kept	keeps	keeping
A	B	C	D	E

in with the

4

boat;	water;	river;	sea;	shore;
A	B	C	D	E

and having a fair, fresh gale of wind, and a smooth, quiet sea,

5

me	myself	I	oneself	own
A	B	C	D	E

made such sail that I believe by the next day, at three o'clock in the afternoon, when I

6

lastly	primary	initial	first	final
A	B	C	D	E

made the land, I could not be

7

but	less	lower	far	many
A	B	C	D	E

than one hundred and fifty miles south of Sallee; quite

8

past	away	from	above	beyond
A	B	C	D	E

the Emperor of Morocco's dominions.

4 minutes

The sentences below contain some **spelling** errors. Each sentence has either **one** error or **no** error. Find the group of words containing the error and circle the corresponding letter beneath. **If there is no error, circle N.**

Sentences: Fiction

1 "You have no apointments scheduled tomorrow," replied her assistant.

A   B   C   D   N

2 The crimnal was found guilty of trespass and attempted burglary.

A   B   C   D   N

3 She was promoted from a supervisior role to a managerial position.

A   B   C   D   N

4 Aparna insisted on bringing her own crockery for hygeine purposes.

A   B   C   D   N

5 The fragrent scent of flowers in bloom signalled the arrival of spring.

A   B   C   D   N

6 She was fatigued after running the marathon with little preparation.

A   B   C   D   N

7 Rhea's impressive performance on her internship earned her a job.

A   B   C   D   N

8 The lion camoflauged itself among the grasslands as it stalked its prey.

A   B   C   D   N

Mixed Test 3 - Punctuation

 **4 minutes**

The passage below contains some errors in the use of **punctuation**, including the use of **capital letters**. On each line, there is either **one** error or **no** error. Find the group of words containing the error and circle the corresponding letter beneath. **If there is no error, circle N.**

Vatican City

1 The smallest state in the world with respect to both population and area; Vatican City is
A   B   C   D   N

2 located within the city of Rome. It is governed by the Pope, with italian and Roman
A   B   C   D   N

3 Catholicism as the official language and religion respectively. the influence of
A   B   C   D   N

4 Catholicism pervades the city and is evident in the two largest tourist attractions, which
A   B   C   D   N

5 are both churches St. Peter's Basilica and the Sistine Chapel. The former is a prominent
A   B   C   D   N

6 place of pilgrimage for Catholics around the world, whilst the latter is known for it's
A   B   C   D   N

7 intricate paintings, which adorn the walls and ceiling. These were painted by
A   B   C   D   N

8 Michelangelo, Botticelli and Roselli, amongst other's, in the 15th and 16th centuries.
A   B   C   D   N

Answers & Explanations

English:

Spelling, Punctuation & Grammar

Multiple Choice

Book 1

Spelling - Exercise 1 - Pluto, page 2

Question	Answer	Explanation
1	C	The incorrectly spelt word is '**initialy**' - the correct spelling is '**initially**'.
2	B	The incorrectly spelt word is '**orbitting**' - the correct spelling is '**orbiting**'.
3	D	The incorrectly spelt word is '**dwarve**' - the correct spelling is '**dwarf**'.
4	B	The incorrectly spelt word is '**similiar**' - the correct spelling is '**similar**'.
5	N	There are no errors - all words are spelt correctly.
6	C	The incorrectly spelt word is '**formel**' - the correct spelling is '**formal**'.
7	B	The incorrectly spelt word is '**desision**' - the correct spelling is '**decision**'.
8	C	The incorrectly spelt word is '**petetions**' - the correct spelling is '**petitions**'.

Spelling - Exercise 2 - Dear Mr Hartley, page 3

Question	Answer	Explanation
1	B	The incorrectly spelt word is '**condem**' - the correct spelling is '**condemn**'.
2	N	There are no errors - all words are spelt correctly.
3	D	The incorrectly spelt word is '**competitons**' - the correct spelling is '**competitions**'.
4	B	The incorrectly spelt word is '**fostor**' - the correct spelling is '**foster**'.
5	B	The incorrectly spelt word is '**beleive**' - the correct spelling is '**believe**'.
6	A	The incorrectly spelt word is '**toowards**' - the correct spelling is '**towards**'.
7	C	The incorrectly spelt word is '**colecting**' - the correct spelling is '**collecting**'.
8	A	The incorrectly spelt word is '**hireing**' - the correct spelling is '**hiring**'.

Spelling - Exercise 3 - The Hound of the Baskervilles, page 4

Question	Answer	Explanation
1	C	The incorrectly spelt word is '**their**' - the correct spelling is '**there**'.
2	N	There are no errors - all words are spelt correctly.
3	C	The incorrectly spelt word is '**jaged**' - the correct spelling is '**jagged**'.
4	B	The incorrectly spelt word is '**iregular**' - the correct spelling is '**irregular**'.
5	C	The incorrectly spelt word is '**definate**' - the correct spelling is '**definite**'.
6	N	There are no errors - all words are spelt correctly.
7	B	The incorrectly spelt word is '**angel**' - the correct spelling is '**angle**'.
8	D	The incorrectly spelt word is '**somersalt**' - the correct spelling is '**somersault**'.

Spelling - Exercise 4 - Sentences: Non-Fiction, page 5

Question	Answer	Explanation
1	D	The incorrectly spelt word is '**anually**' - the correct spelling is '**annually**'.
2	A	The incorrectly spelt word is '**contraray**' - the correct spelling is '**contrary**'.
3	C	The incorrectly spelt word is '**consanants**' - the correct spelling is '**consonants**'.
4	N	There are no errors - all words are spelt correctly.
5	D	The incorrectly spelt word is '**footware**' - the correct spelling is '**footwear**'.
6	N	There are no errors - all words are spelt correctly.
7	B	The incorrectly spelt word is '**nighthood**' - the correct spelling is '**knightnood**'.
8	C	The incorrectly spelt word is '**tounge**' - the correct spelling is '**tongue**'.

Spelling - Exercise 5 - Furry Fiasco, page 6

Question	Answer	Explanation
1	B	The incorrectly spelt word is '**ecxited**' - the correct spelling is '**excited**'.
2	C	The incorrectly spelt word is '**overwelming**' - the correct spelling is '**overwhelming**'.
3	B	The incorrectly spelt word is '**tendancy**' - the correct spelling is '**tendency**'.
4	N	There are no errors - all words are spelt correctly.
5	B	The incorrectly spelt word is '**entranse**' - the correct spelling is '**entrance**'.
6	N	There are no errors - all words are spelt correctly.
7	D	The incorrectly spelt word is '**hatered**' - the correct spelling is '**hatred**'.
8	B	The incorrectly spelt word is '**misgided**' - the correct spelling is '**misguided**'.

Spelling - Exercise 6 - Giant Pandas, page 7

Question	Answer	Explanation
1	D	The incorrectly spelt word is '**distinctiv**' - the correct spelling is '**distinctive**'.
2	N	There are no errors - all words are spelt correctly.
3	A	The incorrectly spelt word is '**bambo**' - the correct spelling is '**bamboo**'.
4	A	The incorrectly spelt word is '**remane**' - the correct spelling is '**remain**'.
5	A	The incorrectly spelt word is '**infastructure**' - the correct spelling is '**infrastructure**'.
6	B	The incorrectly spelt word is '**increace**' - the correct spelling is '**increase**'.
7	N	There are no errors - all words are spelt correctly.
8	D	The incorrectly spelt word is '**vunerable**' - the correct spelling is '**vulnerable**'.

Spelling - Exercise 7 - The Wonderful Wizard of Oz, page 8

Question	Answer	Explanation
1	B	The incorrectly spelt word is '**plummage**' - the correct spelling is '**plumage**'.
2	D	The incorrectly spelt word is '**lowerd**' - the correct spelling is '**lowered**'.
3	B	The incorrectly spelt word is '**tirsome**' - the correct spelling is '**tiresome**'.
4	A	The incorrectly spelt word is '**wizad**' - the correct spelling is '**wizard**'.
5	B	The incorrectly spelt word is '**afriad**' - the correct spelling is '**afraid**'.
6	B	The incorrectly spelt word is '**quiet**' - the correct spelling is '**quite**'.
7	N	There are no errors - all words are spelt **correctly**.
8	C	The incorrectly spelt word is '**sucess**' - the correct spelling is '**success**'.

Spelling - Exercise 8 - Celebrations in Barnford, page 9

Question	Answer	Explanation
1	B	The incorrectly spelt word is '**begining**' - the correct spelling is '**beginning**'.
2	B	The incorrectly spelt word is '**anniversery**' - the correct spelling is '**anniversary**'.
3	B	The incorrectly spelt word is '**comissioned**' - the correct spelling is '**commissioned**'.
4	B	The incorrectly spelt word is '**classifed**' - the correct spelling is '**classified**'.
5	N	There are no errors - all words are spelt correctly.
6	D	The incorrectly spelt word is '**gallary**' - the correct spelling is '**gallery**'.
7	D	The incorrectly spelt word is '**curater**' - the correct spelling is '**curator**'.
8	N	There are no errors - all words are spelt correctly.

Spelling - Exercise 9 - Dad's Secret Weapon, page 10

Question	Answer	Explanation
1	N	There are no errors - all words are spelt correctly.
2	C	The incorrectly spelt word is '**deposeted**' - the correct spelling is '**deposited**'.
3	D	The incorrectly spelt word is '**pasenger**' - the correct spelling is '**passenger**'.
4	N	There are no errors - all words are spelt correctly.
5	B	The incorrectly spelt word is '**phobea**' - the correct spelling is '**phobia**'.
6	D	The incorrectly spelt word is '**tripel**' - the correct spelling is '**triple**'.
7	A	The incorrectly spelt word is '**sunday**' - the correct spelling is '**sundae**'.
8	C	The incorrectly spelt word is '**immedately**' - the correct spelling is '**immediately**'.

Spelling - Exercise 10 - The Adventures of Tom Sawyer, page 11

Question	Answer	Explanation
1	A	The incorrectly spelt word is **'skirtled'** - the correct spelling is **'skirted'**.
2	B	The incorrectly spelt word is **'stabel'** - the correct spelling is **'stable'**.
3	C	The incorrectly spelt word is **'hastend'** - the correct spelling is **'hastened'**.
4	C	The incorrectly spelt word is **'companys'** - the correct spelling is **'companies'**.
5	B	The incorrectly spelt word is **'acording'** - the correct spelling is **'according'**.
6	A	The incorrectly spelt word is **'armys'** - the correct spelling is **'armies'**.
7	C	The incorrectly spelt word is **'condesend'** - the correct spelling is **'condescend'**.
8	N	There are no errors - all words are spelt correctly.

Spelling - Exercise 11 - Anne of Green Gables, page 12

Question	Answer	Explanation
1	N	There are no errors - all words are spelt correctly.
2	C	The incorrectly spelt word is **'disscussed'** - the correct spelling is **'discussed'**.
3	B	The incorrectly spelt word is **'debateing'** - the correct spelling is **'debating'**.
4	B	The incorrectly spelt word is **'sevaral'** - the correct spelling is **'several'**.
5	D	The incorrectly spelt word is **'libary'** - the correct spelling is **'library'**.
6	C	The incorrectly spelt word is **'practiseing'** - the correct spelling is **'practising'**.
7	B	The incorrectly spelt word is **'especialy'** - the correct spelling is **'especially'**.
8	N	There are no errors - all words are spelt correctly.

Spelling - Exercise 12 - Jurassic Park, page 13

Question	Answer	Explanation
1	N	There are no errors - all words are spelt correctly.
2	B	The incorrectly spelt word is **'centered'** - the correct spelling is **'centred'**.
3	C	The incorrectly spelt word is **'enginered'** - the correct spelling is **'engineered'**.
4	D	The incorrectly spelt word is **'prier'** - the correct spelling is **'prior'**.
5	C	The incorrectly spelt word is **'enthuasiasm'** - the correct spelling is **'enthusiasm'**.
6	N	There are no errors - all words are spelt correctly.
7	D	The incorrectly spelt word is **'predecesor'** - the correct spelling is **'predecessor'**.
8	A	The incorrectly spelt word is **'seqeul'** - the correct spelling is **'sequel'**.

Spelling - Exercise 13 - Sentences: Fiction, page 14

Question	Answer	Explanation
1	B	The incorrectly spelt word is '**minuscle**' - the correct spelling is '**minuscule**'.
2	A	The incorrectly spelt word is '**refferee**' - the correct spelling is '**referee**'.
3	N	There are no errors - all words are spelt correctly.
4	C	The incorrectly spelt word is '**liased**' - the correct spelling is '**liaised**'.
5	B	The incorrectly spelt word is '**cemetary**' - the correct spelling is '**cemetery**'.
6	A	The incorrectly spelt word is '**adress**' - the correct spelling is '**address**'.
7	D	The incorrectly spelt word is '**regieme**' - the correct spelling is '**regime**'.
8	C	The incorrectly spelt word is '**concusion**' - the correct spelling is '**concussion**'.

Spelling - Exercise 14 - Treasure Island, page 15

Question	Answer	Explanation
1	D	The incorrectly spelt word is '**explotion**' - the correct spelling is '**explosion**'.
2	N	There are no errors - all words are spelt correctly.
3	A	The incorrectly spelt word is '**steele**' - the correct spelling is '**steel**'.
4	A	The incorrectly spelt word is '**instence**' - the correct spelling is '**instance**'.
5	A	The incorrectly spelt word is '**pursueing**' - the correct spelling is '**pursuing**'.
6	D	The incorrectly spelt word is '**captian**' - the correct spelling is '**captain**'.
7	A	The incorrectly spelt word is '**fugative**' - the correct spelling is '**fugitive**'.
8	C	The incorrectly spelt word is '**intercepeted**' - the correct spelling is '**intercepted**'.

Spelling - Exercise 15 - Motor Neurone Disease, page 16

Question	Answer	Explanation
1	C	The incorrectly spelt word is '**commonley**' - the correct spelling is '**commonly**'.
2	B	The incorrectly spelt word is '**progresive**' - the correct spelling is '**progressive**'.
3	C	The incorrectly spelt word is '**affects**' - the correct spelling is '**effects**'.
4	B	The incorrectly spelt word is '**mucsles**' - the correct spelling is '**muscles**'.
5	B	The incorrectly spelt word is '**paralaysed**' - the correct spelling is '**paralysed**'.
6	N	There are no errors - all words are spelt correctly.
7	B	The incorrectly spelt word is '**diagnozed**' - the correct spelling is '**diagnosed**'.
8	C	The incorrectly spelt word is '**physicsist**' - the correct spelling is '**physicist**'.

Punctuation - Exercise 1 - Through the Looking Glass, page 18

Question	Answer	Explanation
1	N	There are no errors.
2	C	Should be a comma after 'it' because it is the end of direct speech.
3	C	'But' should be capitalised because it is the start of a sentence.
4	B	Should be a comma before 'but' to join the two main clauses together.
5	D	Missing possessive apostrophe in 'TWEEDLEDUM'S'.
6	C	Should be a full stop after 'TWEEDLEDEE' because it is the end of a sentence.
7	D	Misplaced apostrophe in 'can't'. Should indicate omission of the letters 'no'.
8	B	Should be an apostrophe in 'd'you' to indicate omission of the letter 'o'.

Punctuation - Exercise 2 - Hurricanes, page 19

Question	Answer	Explanation
1	A	'Depending' should be capitalised because it is the start of a sentence.
2	D	'Cyclone' should not be capitalised as it is not a proper noun nor the start of a sentence.
3	N	There are no errors.
4	C	Should be a hyphen between 'Saffir' and 'Simpson' to link the two names.
5	C	Should be a comma after 'however' because it is an introductory word.
6	A	Misused apostrophe in 'its' because the possessive pronoun 'its' has no apostrophe.
7	D	Should be no comma after 'strength' because 'Regardless...hurricane' is one clause.
8	D	Misused hyphen: 'outside' is one word.

Punctuation - Exercise 3 - The Emperor's New Clothes, page 20

Question	Answer	Explanation
1	A	'Many' should be capitalised because it is the start of the sentence.
2	B	Should be a full stop, not a question mark, after 'dress'.
3	A	Misused apostrophe in 'soldiers' because there is no possession or omission.
4	N	There are no errors.
5	D	'One' should not be capitalised as it is not a proper noun nor the start of a sentence.
6	B	Should be a comma after 'council' as 'and as of any...council'' is a subordinate clause.
7	A	Should be a closing quotation mark after 'wardrobe' because it is the end of a quotation.
8	D	Misused apostrophe in 'themselves' because there is no possession or omission.

Punctuation - Exercise 4 - Pride and Prejudice, page 21

Question	Answer	Explanation
1	C	Should be a semicolon after 'gentleman-like' to join the two main clauses together.
2	C	Missing possessive apostrophe in 'Maria's'.
3	B	Should be a comma after 'fine' because 'As...fine' is a subordinate clause.
4	N	There are no errors.
5	C	Missing semicolon or comma after 'anyone' to join the two main clauses together.
6	A	'Pride' should not be capitalised as it is not a proper noun nor the start of a sentence.
7	C	Misplaced possessive apostrophe in 'St. James's'. Should be between the two 's's.
8	C	Misused comma: do not separate a verb and its object, e.g. 'give herself'.

Punctuation - Exercise 5 - An Old Treasure, page 22

Question	Answer	Explanation
1	C	Missing possessive apostrophe in 'Lily's'.
2	A	Should be a comma after 'brother' because 'her brother' is extra information.
3	C	Misused hyphen: an adjective and its noun should not be hyphenated.
4	B	Misused apostrophe in 'its' because the possessive pronoun 'its' has no apostrophe.
5	D	Should be no comma after 'agreed' because 'there...now' is a defining relative clause.
6	A	'It' should be capitalised because it is the start of a sentence.
7	N	There are no errors.
8	A	Misplaced apostrophe: it is indicating possession so should be 'Tom's'.

Punctuation - Exercise 6 - Lacrosse, page 23

Question	Answer	Explanation
1	B	Should be a comma after 'century' because 'Well...century' is an introductory phrase.
2	C	Misused apostrophe in 'sports' because there is no possession or omission.
3	B	Should be an inverted comma after 'crosse' to match that before 'la'.
4	A	Misused hyphen: an adjective and its noun should not be hyphenated.
5	N	There are no errors.
6	D	Should be a comma between 'cradle' and 'pass' to separate the items in the list.
7	B	Missing possessive apostrophe in 'team's'.
8	A	'Olympics' should be capitalised because it is a proper noun.

Punctuation - Exercise 7 - Sentences: Fiction, page 24

Question	Answer	Explanation
1	D	Should be a comma after 'cream' to indicate omission of the words 'which is'.
2	A	Should be an apostrophe in 'let's' to indicate omission of the letter 'u'.
3	A	'Your' is the wrong word. Should be 'you're' as in 'Do you think *you are* fearless?'
4	B	Should be a question mark inside the speech marks: "...please?"
5	B	Should be a comma between 'Athens' and 'Greece' to separate the items in the list.
6	B	Misused hyphen between 'hundred' and 'year': don't separate number and adjective.
7	D	Should be an apostrophe in 'hadn't' to indicate omission of the letter 'o'.
8	B	Should be a comma or an exclamation mark inside the speech marks: "...kill me!"

Punctuation - Exercise 8 - Dear Diary, page 25

Question	Answer	Explanation
1	N	There are no errors.
2	A	Should be a comma before 'but' to join the two main clauses together.
3	A	Should be a comma after 'Kevin' because 'my oldest friend' is extra information.
4	C	Should be an apostrophe in 'we're' to indicate omission of the letter 'a'.
5	C	Should be an apostrophe in 'it's' to indicate omission of the letter 'i'.
6	D	Possessive apostrophe in 'twin's' should go after the 's' as there is more than one twin.
7	B	Exclamation mark should be a question mark.
8	N	There are no errors.

Punctuation - Exercise 9 - White Fang, page 26

Question	Answer	Explanation
1	C	Misused apostrophe in 'traces' because there is no possession or omission.
2	D	Misused comma: no comma needed between an adjective and its noun.
3	A	Misused apostrophe in 'its' because the possessive pronoun 'its' has no apostrophe.
4	C	Misused hyphen: an adjective and its noun should not be hyphenated.
5	B	Should be a comma after 'lashed' because 'securely lashed' is extra information.
6	D	'Frying-pan' should not be capitalised as it is not a proper noun nor the start of a sentence.
7	C	Misused comma: no comma needed between two adjectives if 'and' is there.
8	N	There are no errors.

Punctuation - Exercise 10 - Waiting, page 27

Question	Answer	Explanation
1	B	Should be a comma after 'breath' because 'the coarse...into my back' is extra information.
2	D	Misplaced apostrophe in 'wouldn't'. Should indicate omission of the letter 'o'.
3	B	Should be a semicolon after 'me' to join the two main clauses together.
4	N	There are no errors.
5	D	Should be a full stop after 'mouth' because it is the end of the sentence.
6	C	Misused comma after 'past' because you cannot insert 'and' between 'past' and 'few'.
7	N	There are no errors.
8	A	Should be a comma after 'relief' because 'With...relief' is a subordinate clause.

Punctuation - Exercise 11 - The Story of Doctor Doolittle, page 28

Question	Answer	Explanation
1	B	Misused quotation marks: use quotation marks to indicate a direct quotation.
2	A	'House' should not be capitalised as it is not a proper noun nor the start of a sentence.
3	B	Missing possessive apostrophe in 'butcher's'.
4	B	Should be a closing speech mark after 'nuisance' because it is the end of direct speech.
5	D	Full stop should be a question mark.
6	A	Misused apostrophe in 'themselves' because there is no possession or omission.
7	N	There are no errors.
8	B	Should be a comma after 'Too-Too' because 'Too-Too' is extra information.

Punctuation - Exercise 12 - Muhammad Ali, page 29

Question	Answer	Explanation
1	A	Should be an opening quotation mark before 'Float' because it is the start of a quotation.
2	C	Misplaced possessive apostrophe in 'Ali's'.
3	B	Should be no comma after 'win' because 'Following...Olympics' is one subordinate clause.
4	A	Should be a comma after 'flourished' as 'culminating...champion' is a subordinate clause.
5	C	'Title' should not be capitalised because it is not a proper noun nor the start of a sentence.
6	A	Should be no comma after 'ring' because 'which...Freedom' is defining relative clause.
7	N	There are no errors.
8	B	Missing possessive apostrophe in 'People's'.

Punctuation - Exercise 13 - Sentences: Non-Fiction, page 30

Question	Answer	Explanation
1	B	Should be a comma after 'woodwind' to separate the items in the list.
2	C	Should be no comma after 'France' as there's no need to separate 'France' from 'by land'.
3	D	'Greek' should be capitalised. All languages are proper nouns.
4	A	'Your' is the wrong word. Should be 'you're' as in '*You are* born...'
5	D	Should be an inverted comma before 'Teddy' to match the inverted comma after it.
6	N	There are no errors.
7	A	Missing possessive apostrophe in 'world's'.
8	D	Should be no comma after 'waged' as there's no need to separate 'waged' from 'from...'.

Punctuation - Exercise 14 - Overcooked, page 31

Question	Answer	Explanation
1	N	There are no errors.
2	A	Should be an apostrophe in 'shouldn't' to indicate omission of the letter 'o'.
3	B	Comma should either be an exclamation mark, or 'why' should not be capitalised.
4	N	There are no errors.
5	C	Should be no comma after 'of' as there's no need to separate 'of' from 'his cousin'.
6	D	Should be no comma after 'him' as there's no need to separate 'him' from 'in his tracks'.
7	D	Should be a full stop after 'chuckled' because it is the end of a sentence.
8	C	Question mark should be a full stop or an exclamation mark.

Punctuation - Exercise 15 - Titanic, page 32

Question	Answer	Explanation
1	C	Full stop should be a question mark.
2	D	Misplaced apostrophe in 'you're'. Should indicate omission of the letter 'a'.
3	N	There are no errors.
4	B	Misused semicolon because 'a luxury...maiden voyage from...' is one subordinate clause.
5	B	'Constructed' should be capitalised because it is the start of a sentence.
6	B	Misused brackets: brackets enclose extra information not essential to the sentence.
7	N	There are no errors.
8	D	Misused hyphen: use to join words as compound adjectives, verbs or nouns.

Grammar & Word Choice - Exercise 1 - Backgammon, page 34

Question	Answer	Explanation
1	D	The correct word is 'globally': 'Popularised globally in the late 20th century…'
2	C	The correct word is 'Whilst': 'Whilst the exact origins are unknown…'
3	B	The correct word is 'believed': '…it is believed to be a direct descendent…'
4	A	The correct word is 'involves': 'Backgammon is a two-player game that involves rolling…'
5	B	The correct word is 'around': '…moving one's counters around the board.'
6	D	The correct word is 'remove': '…for the individual to remove all their pieces…'
7	E	The correct word is 'before': '…all their pieces from the board before their opponent…'
8	B	The correct word is 'dependent': 'Success in the game is dependent on not only…'

Grammar & Word Choice - Exercise 2 - Tricky Trailers, page 35

Question	Answer	Explanation
1	C	The correct word is 'loathed': '…she absolutely loathed the trailers…'
2	E	The correct word is 'deliberately': 'She was sure that they were deliberately long…'
3	C	The correct word is 'before': '…would finish their popcorn before the film started…'
4	C	The correct word is 'was': 'The price of popcorn was already extortionate…'
5	E	The correct group of words is 'fall into': '…she was determined not to fall into that trap…'
6	D	The correct group of words is 'to delay': '…this time she was going to delay going…'
7	D	The correct word is 'Unluckily,': 'Unluckily, she chose the one day…'
8	B	The correct word is 'stopped': '…when the trailers stopped early…'

Grammar & Word Choice - Exercise 3 - The Wind in the Willows, page 36

Question	Answer	Explanation
1	C	The correct word is 'content': 'The Mole had to be content with this.'
2	D	The correct word is 'brought': '…every day brought its amusements.'
3	B	The correct word is 'summer': '…it was not till summer was long over…'
4	E	The correct word is 'them': '…cold and frost and miry ways kept them much indoors…'
5	E	The correct word is 'outside': '…the swollen river raced past outside their windows…'
6	C	The correct word is 'found': '…he found his thoughts dwelling…'
7	D	The correct word is 'much': '…his thoughts dwelling again with much persistence…'
8	B	The correct word is 'by': '…who lived his own life by himself…'

Grammar & Word Choice - Exercise 4 - Trams, page 37

Question	Answer	Explanation
1	E	The correct word is 'that': 'Trams are public transportation vehicles **that** run…'
2	C	The correct word is 'established': 'A network of **established** trams forms…'
3	B	The correct word is 'these': '…and **these** travel through…'
4	D	The correct word is 'Despite': '**Despite** continued investment…'
5	C	The correct word is 'compared': '…when **compared** to buses and automobiles…'
6	C	The correct word is 'consider': '…certain countries still **consider** them cumbersome…'
7	B	The correct group of words is 'has been': '…the infrastructure **has been** refined…'
8	D	The correct word is 'efficient': '…with a fast, flexible and energy-**efficient** mode…'

Grammar & Word Choice - Exercise 5 - Piled-Up Paperwork, page 38

Question	Answer	Explanation
1	C	The correct word is 'despair': 'Harold groaned in **despair** at the sight of…'
2	D	The correct word is 'up': '…all the paperwork that had built **up** on his desk…'
3	E	The correct word is 'hardly': 'This was why he **hardly** ever went on holiday…'
4	C	The correct word is 'handle': '…always said they could **handle** the office without him…'
5	C	The correct word is 'yesterday': 'This time **yesterday** he had been…'
6	B	The correct word is 'lying': '…he had been **lying** on a sandy beach…'
7	C	The correct word is 'calendar,': 'Peering down at his **calendar,** he gave a resigned sigh…'
8	C	The correct word is 'next': '…only three months until his **next** holiday.'

Grammar & Word Choice - Exercise 6 - Dear Uncle Bernard, page 39

Question	Answer	Explanation
1	C	The correct group of words is 'sent me': '…for the card and money you **sent me**…'
2	B	The correct group of words is 'I have': '**I have** been saving up…'
3	B	The correct word is 'should': '…your gift means I **should** be able…'
4	D	The correct word is 'so': '…to give me more chores **so** I can earn a little extra…'
5	D	The correct word is 'refuse': '…but I **refuse** to throw the bins out…'
6	E	The correct word is 'you': 'I was really upset that **you** couldn't come to my…'
7	E	The correct word is 'in': '…Auntie Ellen said you're busy **in** Egypt…'
8	C	The correct group of words is 'Lots of': '**Lots of** love, Your favourite nephew'

Grammar & Word Choice - Exercise 7 - The Elves and the Shoemaker, page 40

Question	Answer	Explanation
1	B	The correct word is 'amidst': '...his heart light amidst all his troubles...'
2	D	The correct word is 'cares': '...left all his cares to Heaven...'
3	A	The correct word is 'morning': 'In the morning after he had said his prayers...'
4	C	The correct word is 'stood': '...there stood the shoes all ready made...'
5	D	The correct word is 'upon': '...there stood the shoes all ready made, upon the table.'
6	B	The correct word is 'odd': '...knew not what to say or think at such an odd thing...'
7	B	The correct word is 'not': '...there was not one false stitch in the whole job...'
8	E	The correct word is 'neat': '...all was so neat and true, that it was quite a masterpiece.'

Grammar & Word Choice - Exercise 8 - The NHS, page 41

Question	Answer	Explanation
1	D	The correct word is 'operating': '...the healthcare system currently operating in...'
2	E	The correct word is 'fundamental': '...built upon three fundamental principles...'
3	C	The correct group of words is 'was free': '...that it was free at the point of use...'
4	C	The correct word is 'in': '...these principles remain in place...'
5	E	The correct word is 'pressure': '...has found itself under significant pressure in recent...'
6	B	The correct word is 'increase': 'With an ageing population, an increase in chronic...'
7	E	The correct word is 'are': '...its services are overstretched.'
8	B	The correct word is 'slows': 'As spending on healthcare slows down year on year...'

Grammar & Word Choice - Exercise 9 - Sentences: Fiction, page 42

Question	Answer	Explanation
1	B	The correct word is 'nothing': 'There was nothing on the table when we left...'
2	C	The correct group of words is 'had sold': '...all the tickets had sold out the week before.'
3	B	The correct group of words is 'has finished': '...after she has finished all her homework.'
4	D	The correct word is 'Since': 'Since she fell off her bike...'
5	C	The correct word is '"Who's': '"Who's that player in the red shirt?"'
6	C	The correct word is 'conflicted': '...as it conflicted with her basketball practice.'
7	B	The correct word is 'over': 'The ball soared over the wooden fence...'
8	E	The correct word is 'few': 'There were too few students there...'

Grammar & Word Choice - Exercise 10 - A Christmas Carol, page 43

Question	Answer	Explanation
1	C	The correct word is 'at': 'But he was a tight-fisted hand at the grindstone, Scrooge!'
2	D	The correct word is 'covetous': '...grasping, scraping, clutching, covetous old sinner!'
3	B	The correct word is 'which': 'Hard and sharp as flint, from which no steel...'
4	E	The correct word is 'secret': '...secret and self-contained...'
5	E	The correct word is 'and': '...self-contained, and solitary as an oyster.'
6	D	The correct word is 'froze': 'The cold within him froze his old features...'
7	E	The correct word is 'made': '...stiffened his gait; made his eyes red...'
8	C	The correct word is 'spoke': '...and spoke out shrewdly in his grating voice.'

Grammar & Word Choice - Exercise 11 - Google, page 44

Question	Answer	Explanation
1	D	The correct word is 'company': 'Google Inc. is a multi-national company...'
2	C	The correct word is 'creation': 'Since its creation in 1998...'
3	B	The correct word is 'offer': '..the company has expanded to offer more than 50...'
4	D	The correct group of words is 'as well as': '...books and maps, as well as the mobile...'
5	C	The correct word is 'capable': 'It is capable of handling over a billion search requests...'
6	E	The correct word is 'analysing': '...which requires analysing millions of pages a second.'
7	B	The correct word is 'willing': 'The founders were willing to sell it for...'
8	D	The correct word is 'most': '...it is now the world's most valuable brand...'

Grammar & Word Choice - Exercise 12 - Sentences: Non-Fiction, page 45

Question	Answer	Explanation
1	D	The correct word is 'named': 'The pavlova, a meringue-based cake, is named after...'
2	B	The correct word is 'most': 'Wimbledon is the oldest and most prestigious...'
3	E	The correct word is 'produced': '...William Shakespeare, produced a plethora of plays...'
4	B	The correct word is 'widely': 'The moon landing is widely regarded as NASA's...'
5	A	The correct word is 'remains': '...for Leonardo da Vinci's the *Mona Lisa* remains a...'
6	C	The correct group of words is 'for whom': 'Boudica was a Celtic queen, for whom...'
7	E	The correct word is 'into': 'The Harry Potter books have been translated into 75...'
8	C	The correct word is 'lasting': 'After an exhausting voyage lasting 1,742 days...'

Grammar & Word Choice - Exercise 13 - The Secret Garden, page 46

Question	Answer	Explanation
1	E	The correct word is '**imagine**': '...most mysterious-looking place anyone could **imagine**.'
2	C	The correct word is '**covered**': 'The high walls which shut it in were **covered**...'
3	D	The correct word is '**matted**': '...were so thick they were **matted** together.'
4	E	The correct word is '**because**': '...they were roses **because** she had seen a great many...'
5	B	The correct word is '**ground**': 'All the **ground** was covered with grass...'
6	C	The correct word is '**clumps**': '...out of it grew **clumps** of bushes...'
7	B	The correct word is '**surely**': '...which were **surely** rose-bushes...'
8	B	The correct word is '**were**': '...if they **were** alive.'

Grammar & Word Choice - Exercise 14 - The Great Wall of China, page 47

Question	Answer	Explanation
1	A	The correct word is '**construction**': '...the **construction** of the Great Wall dates...'
2	D	The correct word is '**commonly**': 'Although **commonly** mistaken as one long wall...'
3	C	The correct word is '**comprise**': '...the Great Wall does in fact **comprise** several walls...'
4	B	The correct word is '**successive**': '...built by **successive** dynasties.'
5	C	The correct word is '**its**': '...remnants of **its** previous function...'
6	E	The correct word is '**defence**': '...its previous function as a **defence** mechanism...'
7	C	The correct word is '**along**': 'Dotted **along** the wall are watchtowers...'
8	D	The correct word is '**against**': '...once used for surveillance **against** invasions...'

Grammar & Word Choice - Exercise 15 - Tarzan of the Apes, page 48

Question	Answer	Explanation
1	D	The correct word is '**two**': 'Not thirty paces behind the **two** she crouched...'
2	E	The correct word is '**Cautiously**': '**Cautiously** she moved a great padded paw...'
3	B	The correct word is '**forward**': '...she moved a great padded paw **forward**, noiselessly...'
4	C	The correct word is '**her**': 'Thus she advanced; **her** belly low...'
5	D	The correct word is '**surface**': '...almost touching the **surface** of the ground...'
6	B	The correct word is '**spring**': '...a great cat preparing to **spring** upon its prey.'
7	E	The correct word is '**within**': 'Now she was **within** ten feet...'
8	A	The correct word is '**drew**': '...carefully she **drew** her hind feet well up beneath her...'

Mixed Test 1

Spelling - Heidi, page 50

Question	Answer	Explanation
1	C	The incorrectly spelt word is '**asending**' - the correct spelling is '**ascending**'.
2	B	The incorrectly spelt word is '**were**' - the correct spelling is '**where**'.
3	A	The incorrectly spelt word is '**grasing**' - the correct spelling is '**grazing**'.
4	D	The incorrectly spelt word is '**folowed**' - the correct spelling is '**followed**'.
5	N	There are no errors.
6	C	The incorrectly spelt word is '**uncomfortible**' - the correct spelling is '**uncomfortable**'.
7	C	The incorrectly spelt word is '**strenth**' - the correct spelling is '**strength**'.
8	B	The incorrectly spelt word is '**envyously**' - the correct spelling is '**enviously**'.

Punctuation - My Time Had Come, page 51

Question	Answer	Explanation
1	B	Misused comma: do not separate the subject from its verb.
2	A	'Don't' should be capitalised because it is the start of direct speech.
3	B	Missing possessive apostrophe in 'Mum's'.
4	C	Misused comma after 'deep': no comma needed between an adjective and its noun.
5	C	Misused hyphen: use to join words as compound adjectives, verbs or nouns.
6	B	Should be a semicolon or colon after 'again' to join the two main clauses together.
7	C	Should be an apostrophe in 'I'd' to indicate omission of the letters 'ha'.
8	N	There are no errors.

Grammar & Word Choice - Pokémon, page 52

Question	Answer	Explanation
1	C	The correct word is 'unlikely': '...it is **unlikely** that he anticipated just how popular...'
2	B	The correct group of words is 'would be.': '...the fictional characters **would be.**'
3	B	The correct word is 'franchise': '...the Pokémon media **franchise** now spans not only...'
4	C	The correct word is 'but': '...the original video games, **but** also trading card games...'
5	B	The correct word is 'recently,': '...and most **recently,** a mobile, augmented-reality...'
6	A	The correct word is 'modes': 'Despite the evolution in **modes** of play...'
7	B	The correct word is 'same,': '...the concept remains the **same,** Pokémon trainers...'
8	C	The correct word is 'their': '...must catch and train **their** Pokémon in battle.'

Mixed Test 2

Punctuation - The Prince and the Pauper, page 54

Question	Answer	Explanation
1	A	Missing possessive apostrophe in 'Tom's'.
2	A	Should be a full stop after 'delight' and 'everything' should be capitalised.
3	B	Should be a comma after 'good' to separate the two interchangeable adjectives.
4	C	'The' should be capitalised because it is the start of a sentence.
5	N	There are no errors.
6	A	'London' should be capitalised because it is a proper noun.
7	C	'Prince' should not be capitalised as it is not a proper noun nor the start of a sentence.
8	D	'How' should be capitalised because it is the start of direct speech.

Grammar & Word Choice - Lost!, page 55

Question	Answer	Explanation
1	B	The correct word is 'with': 'A large black Labrador **with** noticeable white streaks…'
2	E	The correct group of words is 'last seen': 'She was **last seen** in State Park…'
3	B	The correct word is 'an': '...inscribed with **an** 'H'.'
4	A	The correct group of words is '**be carrying**': '...and may **be carrying** a red spotted ball.'
5	E	The correct word is 'of': 'There is a reward **of** £200 available for anyone who finds her…'
6	E	The correct word is 'smaller': '...and a **smaller** sum of £50 for anyone…'
7	B	The correct word is 'If': '**If** found, please call us on…'
8	B	The correct word is 'leave': '...or **leave** a text message.'

Spelling - Global Warming, page 56

Question	Answer	Explanation
1	C	The incorrectly spelt word is '**averege**' - the correct spelling is '**average**'.
2	B	The incorrectly spelt word is '**atmasphere**' - the correct spelling is '**atmosphere**'.
3	A	The incorrectly spelt word is '**naturelly**' - the correct spelling is '**naturally**'.
4	A	The incorrectly spelt word is '**acelerating**' - the correct spelling is '**accelerating**'.
5	D	The incorrectly spelt word is '**dioxede**' - the correct spelling is '**dioxide**'.
6	N	There are no errors.
7	N	There are no errors.
8	D	The incorrectly spelt word is '**dessert**' - the correct spelling is '**desert**'.

Mixed Test 3

Grammar & Word Choice - Robinson Crusoe, page 58

Question	Answer	Explanation
1	E	The correct word is 'grew': 'But as soon as it grew dusk in the evening…'
2	B	The correct word is 'and': '…I changed my course, and steered directly south…'
3	A	The correct word is 'keep': '…that I might keep in with…'
4	E	The correct word is 'shore;': '…I might keep in with the shore; and having a fair…'
5	C	The correct word is 'I': '…and a smooth, quiet sea, I made such sail that I believe…'
6	D	The correct word is 'first': '…when I first made the land…'
7	B	The correct word is 'less': '…I could not be less than one hundred and fifty miles south…'
8	E	The correct word is 'beyond': '…quite beyond the Emperor of Morocco's dominions.'

Spelling - Sentences: Fiction, page 59

Question	Answer	Explanation
1	A	The incorrectly spelt word is 'apointments' - the correct spelling is 'appointments'.
2	A	The incorrectly spelt word is 'crimnal' - the correct spelling is 'criminal'.
3	B	The incorrectly spelt word is 'supervisior' - the correct spelling is 'supervisor'.
4	D	The incorrectly spelt word is 'hygeine' - the correct spelling is 'hygiene'.
5	A	The incorrectly spelt word is 'fragrent' - the correct spelling is 'fragrant'.
6	N	There are no errors.
7	N	There are no errors.
8	A	The incorrectly spelt word is 'camoflauged' - the correct spelling is 'camouflaged'.

Punctuation - Vatican City, page 60

Question	Answer	Explanation
1	D	Semicolon should be a comma because the introductory clause cannot be a sentence.
2	D	'Italian' should be capitalised. All languages are proper nouns.
3	D	'The' should be capitalised as it is the start of a sentence.
4	N	There are no errors.
5	A	Missing colon after 'churches' because it is introducing the following items.
6	D	Misused apostrophe in 'its' because the possessive pronoun 'its' has no apostrophe.
7	N	There are no errors.
8	C	Misused apostrophe in 'others' because there is no possession or omission.

Other Titles in the First Past The Post® Series

English: Practice Papers (GL)

These books provide real exam practice via four timed tests. These are tailored towards the Granada Learning (GL) English assessments but provide invaluable practice for all exam boards. Each test comprises a comprehension section and a spelling, punctuation and grammar section, reflecting the likely make-up of the real exam. Full answers and explanations are included.

Each test can be marked and evaluated via our Peer-Compare™ Online system, which assesses the candidate's performance anonymously on a question-by-question basis. This helps identify areas for improvement and benchmarks the candidate's score against that of others who have taken the same tests.